Cultural
Research Center

 ARIZONA CHRISTIAN
UNIVERSITY

Dear Debbie,

Thank you for your generous donation and your support of the ongoing work of Dr. George Barna and the Cultural Research Center at Arizona Christian University.

As a token of our appreciation, please enjoy this copy of Dr. Barna's newest book, *Helping Millennials Thrive: Practical Wisdom for a Generation in Crisis* – featuring research from Dr. George Barna, with contributions from national experts and ministry leaders.

We are grateful for your partnership with us in the battle for the hearts, minds, and souls of America, and for your commitment to helping advance Biblical Worldview.

May the insights and analysis you read inspire you to engage with the Millennial Generation, and continue making disciples wherever the Lord has called you.

Yours for worldview transformation,

Tracy F. Munsil, Ph.D.

Helping Millennials Thrive

Practical Wisdom for a Generation in Crisis

Featuring Research from George Barna

----

with Contributions from National Leaders and Experts

Foreword by Len Munsil

Edited by Tracy F. Munsil, Ph.D.

Helping Millennials Thrive:
Practical Wisdom for a Generation in Crisis

ISBN: 9781735776330 (paperback)
ISBN: 9781735776378 (ebook)

Requests for permissions should be addressed to:
Arizona Christian University Press
1 W. Firestorm Way
Glendale, AZ 85306

Printed in the United States of America

The first part of this book is a reprint of:

Millennials In America: New Insights into the
Generation of Growing Influence

A Research Report by George Barna,
Cultural Research Center at Arizona Christian University
Published by Arizona Christian University Press, 2021

A Project of:

Foundations of Freedom is a peer-to-peer platform where believers in
traditional American Values unite, maximizing our collective influence and
impact on society.

Cultural
Research Center

The Cultural Research Center at Arizona Christian University exists to
advance the Kingdom of God by conducting culture and worldview studies that provide research and resources to inform and mobilize strategic
engagement in cultural transformation.

We thank Foundations of Freedom for their generous
support of this research.

Part I: The Research

PART I: THE RESEARCH
Millennials in America: Millennials in America:
New Insights into the Generation of Growing Influence
George Barna

TABLE OF CONTENTS

Part II: Other Voices

Foreword by Len Munsil

President, Arizona Christian University

My wife, Dr. Tracy Munsil, is the executive drector of the Cultural Research Center at Arizona Christian University and editor of this book. But before she earned her Ph.D. and returned to full-time work outside the home, she gave birth to our eight children between January of 1987 and May of 1996.

That means two things—yes, she was essentially pregnant for most of our first decade of marriage—but more significantly for this research and this book, that means that all eight of our now-adult children are members of the Millennial Generation.

So, we have not only a professional interest but a deeply personal fascination with understanding the unique challenges and experiences that have shaped this extraordinary and influential generation.

I spent my first decade as a university president overseeing a campus comprised predominantly of Millennials. Today, Millennials are a sizable percentage of the Arizona Christian University workforce.

Millennials have been much maligned and stereotyped. Do a quick search and you will see them described as lazy, entitled, job-hopping, smart-phone addicted, politically correct, and overly sensitive snowflakes.

Having watched Millennials grow to adulthood—not only our children and their friends, but as students at ACU and now as employees—I have a very different picture of Millennials.

Now the largest living generation of Americans, Millennials not only are driving consumer choices and cultural conversations, they are moving into significant positions of leadership in our nation.

From my perspective, one of the most compelling elements of the Millennial Generation is their deep desire to be a positive influence, to build relationships and community, to improve society, and ultimately do something significant with their lives.

For ACU students grounded and guided by biblical faith, I have seen these Millennial characteristics propel our graduates into positions of influence for good by building families, nonprofits, and businesses—serving, encouraging, and building community wherever they go.

The research contained in this report, collected and summarized by my friend Dr. George Barna—an indefatigable national treasure for the body of Christ— can help us by revealing challenges and opportunities for this generation.

Barna's research through the years has been vital in helping Christians to understand and measure the influences and motivations within the body of Christ.

This study is no different. After this research was released, we hosted a series of live national webinars responding to various elements of the research, sponsored by our friends at Foundations of Freedom. I had the opportunity to moderate these webinars, where we brought in national experts to react to the findings in the Millennial report and, most importantly, to offer thoughts and possible solutions to some of the challenges facing this generation.

Many of those national experts have contributed to this book, and we are grateful for their participation.

As you read and consider the research and the wisdom offered by our contributors, I hope you will be challenged and encouraged to consider your role—whether you are a Millennial or from a previous or subsequent generation—in helping this unique and powerful generation to flourish.

Len Munsil, B.S., J.D.
President
Arizona Christian University

From the Editor, Tracy F.Munsil, Ph.D.

Many of us among Baby Boomers have long suspected we have failed the Millennial Generation. Young people deconstructing the faith of their upbringing. Parents who tell stories of adult children walking away from the church. We've seen the signs all around us for quite some time. Now, the research in this book from Dr. George Barna gives us the numbers.

When we saw the initial findings from the groundbreaking study, *Millennials In America: New Insights Into the Generation of Growing Influence*, we were stunned. Millennials are facing critical (perhaps even existential) crises in four defining areas of life:

- **RELATIONSHIPS:** Millennials struggle in relationships. They find it difficult to trust others and go out of their way to avoid relational conflict. When asked what changes would make their lives better, one of the top answers was "better, deeper friendships."

- **MENTAL HEALTH:** A surprisingly high number of Millennials face significant mental health struggles. A majority often feel anxious, depressed, or fearful and acknowledged some degree of emotional fragility or even mental illness.

- **MEANING AND PURPOSE:** Three-fourths of Millennials say they are searching for meaning and purpose in their lives.

- **FAITH:** A record-breaking 40% of young adults are "Don'ts"—they don't believe, don't know, and don't care whether God exists. Only one-third of Millennials claim to believe in God. And only 4% of Millennials have a biblical worldview—the lowest level of biblical worldview understanding of any generation since first measured more than 25 years ago by Dr. Barna.

This research identifies some very real and very deep problems. Our desire in publishing this book is to not only share Dr. Barna's findings to help better understand this generation, but also to bring together key voices who can help identify *real solutions*—practical ways to support, encourage, and help the next generation experience all God has for them.

We've strategically designed *Helping Millennials Thrive* as a resource that connects the most thorough and detailed research available from veteran researcher Dr. George Barna, with practical solutions for addressing the deep needs of the Millennial Generation.

How this book came about

When the research was first released, Foundations of Freedom, who commissioned the research, offered to host a virtual Millennial Panel to share the new data. Dr. Barna led the first panel, presenting highlights from his research. What followed was a rich discussion by distinguished panelists, moderated by Arizona Christian University President Len Munsil. Many of the panelists are included among the contributors to this text. We came away from that event knowing there was much more to share and discuss.

Shortly after, leaders from Foundations of Freedom, the Cultural Research Center, and Arizona Christian University spent time debriefing, reviewing, discussing, and praying. We were deeply moved by the sobering generational portrait emerging from Dr. Barna's Millennial research. And we knew we'd only scratched the surface in facilitating conversation and offering solutions.

We kicked off 2022 with three more panels, bringing together more national experts and ministry leaders to focus with greater depth on each of the four key findings—relational and mental health, lack of meaning and purpose, and spiritual crisis and loss of the biblical worldview. The Millennial Panels can be found on the website of the Cultural Research Center (www.CulturalResearchCenter.com).

Even after those events, we knew the project wasn't done.

So this book was created to share Dr. Barna's research findings more broadly and continue fueling a national dialogue around the critical question: "What can be done?"

How this book is structured

As we developed this book, we wanted to connect the research with practical, real-world solutions from leading experts and ministry leaders from around the nation.

That's why in Part One, you will find Dr. Barna's groundbreaking research, *Millennials in America: New Insights Into the Generation of Growing Influence.* You'll find more about the four main themes of the research—relationships, mental health, meaning and purpose, and faith—and you'll also have access to the full report of Dr. Barna's deep, incredibly detailed analysis of the hearts and minds of the Millennial Generation. Our hope is that presenting the research in its entirety offers unique points of connection for understanding and engaging with the Millennials in your life.

Part Two features contributions from 11 national leaders and experts, each sharing insights and practical solutions for addressing the daunting crises identified in the research. Each participated in the Millennial panels, and here they expand and deepen their responses regarding how to support and encourage Millennials and to help their generation thrive.

This part of the book begins with a powerful Millennial voice, Dr. JoAnna Dias. In her counseling ministry, Dias is in the trenches daily with Millennials, as they grapple through the challenges identified in the research.

In "A Christian Formational Approach to Supporting Millennials," Dias takes us back to the basics—helping Millennials to know their true identity in Christ. But like most journeys to restore faith, Dias challenges us to begin with our own hearts. By focusing on what she calls the "Christian Formational Approach," Dias calls us to reenergize our own sense of self and hope in Jesus, which will enable us to encourage Millennials as they seek to develop a stronger sense of identity in Christ. Full of compassionate reminders of the deep needs of Millennials, Dias shares practical tools for "meeting them in their hurt, despair, and anger with words of life and love."

Following Dias are three giants of the faith—generational fathers whose contributions share prophetic vision for the Millennial Generation.

International ministry leader Dr. Che' Ahn reminds us that no generation since World War II has faced the shaking experienced by the Millennial Generation. In "A Shaken Generation: Returning the Hearts of Millennials to Jesus," Ahn incisively argues that Millennials are facing an unprecedented convergence of crises—the COVID pandemic, the disintegration of the family and the rise of fatherlessness, and a "lukewarm" church. Ahn asks, "What will be the result of all this shaking?" He turns to Malachi 4:5-7, arguing that the shaking will lead to revival—but we must do our part. He offers a practical five-point strategy for partnering with God to bring revival to the Millennial Generation and the nation.

National Hispanic leader Samuel Rodriguez casts a similarly powerful prophetic vision of revival for the Millennial Generation. In "Restoring Millennials with the Agenda of the Lamb," Rodriguez calls out "complacent, comfortable, cowardly Christianity," and offers seven clear propositions in his "Agenda of the Lamb," for a restored church capable of reaching and bringing revival to the Millennial Generation.

In "Asleep at the Wheel," Dr. Raleigh Washington calls on the family, the church, and Christian universities to be bold voices for biblical truth. While the church has been sleeping in its role of speaking truth, a toxic culture has engulfed Millennials. Washington considers the influence cultural forces such as Black Lives Matter, Critical Race Theory, and the idea of systemic racism have had on the Millennial Generation. In his powerful wake-up call, Pastor Washington reminds us that the deep racial and social divisions rocking the Millennial Generation and our nation can only be overcome through unity in Jesus Christ.

The next three contributions grapple with the crisis of the loss of truth in the Millennial Generation.

Radio commentator and author Lucas Miles analyzes the many false messages in American culture (radical environmentalism, Critical Race Theory, gender identity, and Socialism) that lead Millennials to embrace empty substitutes instead of the truth of God. In "An Unchanging Something," Miles responds to each of these false narratives with biblical truth. But he reminds us that just as the Athenians in Acts 17 were seeking the "unknown god," Millennials are passionately seeking higher things. They long for truth in a culture that has no real truth to offer. As Miles sees it, the challenge is to steer Millennials' passions back to Christ and find new ways to introduce them to Jesus—the "unchanging something" their generation seeks.

Author and apologist Jason Jimenez finds that the denial of objective truth has created a crisis of faith among Millennials, which (tragically) leads them even further from truth. In "Bringing Hope to the Spiritual Disillusionment of Millennials," Jimenez shares seven reasons Millennials say they've abandoned the Christian faith, then offers a relational guide for bringing Millennials back, including practical tips such hosting a Bible study, modeling Christian living, and conversing on the basics of the faith.

Pastor and radio host Isaac Crockett shares his personal ministry experiences, as he points to the need for an authentic witness of the presence of God in our lives. In "What to Do with a Generation that Rejects Absolute Truth," Crockett prompts us to first turn inward to get our own hearts and worldview right, before turning outward to minister to Millennials. For Crockett, personal, spirit-led investment in the lives of individual Millennials is the path for overcoming the rejection of truth by the next Generation.

The next two contributions focus on the basic starting point of any effort with Millennials—restoring relationships. As the research shows, Millennials deeply desire to develop and improve their relationships.

Nationally renowned relationship expert Ken Sande shares from decades of relational ministry in "Feed Millennials' Hunger for Relationships." Starved for authentic relationships and community, Sande shares the power of personal example and offers proven practical tools for building relationships that Millennials deeply desire.

One of the most surprising findings was that 39% of the youngest Millennials (18 to 24) identify as LGBTQ+. Ministry leader Garry Ingraham addresses this phenomenon from experience and with compassion in his contribution, "Building Trust and Restoring Hope." Ingraham shares how parents of Millennials missed the mark in passing down a Christian faith that enabled Millennials to navigate the culture. Turning to the example of King Josiah in 2 Kings, Ingraham shows how the church can rebuild a community of love, trust, and authenticity able to nurture and minister to the Millennial Generation—and beyond.

Helping Millennials Thrive closes with a look forward—to how Christian higher education can help rebuild and restore the nation's biblical foundation. Christian colleges and universities are uniquely positioned to offer the authentic community so desired by younger generations, and to shape the vibrant, engaged faith that Millennials missed. The hope is that this cycle of lost generations can be broken in our Christian colleges and universities.

William Jessup University President John Jackson shares his heart and his powerful strategy for the next generation. In "Millennials in America—Weeping Now and Joy is Coming!" Jackson models how to pray for revival. To bring about what he calls a "Second Reformation" through younger generations, Jackson identifies "Five Smooth Stones" to overcome the daunting cultural challenges facing younger Christians, just as David's stones were able to fell the giant of his day.

And finally, ACU Bible professor Jeffrey Phillips amplifies the importance of community among young people. Sharing his own campus ministry experience in "Helping Millennials Through Authentic, Purpose-Driven Community," Phillips encourages us to learn the lessons of the Millennial Generation and apply them to college students today, by strategically focusing on saturating them in authentic community and shaping their biblical worldview while in college.

Closing thoughts

When I read the Millennial research, I'm led to pray for the prodigals in the Millennial Generation. I've spoken with many parents in my generation, who raised their children in the faith, who regularly attended church as a family, who home educated their kids or sent them to Christian high schools. Their hearts are broken. The statistics in the Millennial research are the sons and daughters of my generation. I hear the stories of parents, watching the brokenness in their children's generation, in their children's lives.

So many Millennials have walked away from the faith, swept away by the powerful messages of this anti-God culture. This book describes that Prodigal generation—but also offers a way back to human flourishing.

Part I: The Research

*Millennials in America: New Insights
into the Generation of Growing Influence*

———

BY GEORGE BARNA
DIRECTOR OF RESEARCH, CULTURAL RESEARCH CENTER
AT ARIZONA CHRISTIAN UNIVERSITY

MILLENNIALS IN AMERICA

A Welcome From the Researcher, George Barna

Good research both answers important questions and raises new ones. The goal of such research is to inform and guide decision-makers to lead as wisely, efficiently, and effectively as possible.

I believe the research described in this book can help you do that.

Conducted at the request of Foundations of Freedom, this study addresses various aspects of the life of the Millennial Generation. Why them? Because Millennials, while much studied, have also been much misunderstood and maligned. Yet, with all of the members of that generation now adults, they are entering the defining period of any generation—the high-energy, high-stakes, and high impact years of their 20s and 30s. This season will define the cohort once and for all—and, in all likelihood, will determine the course of our nation for many years to come.

In that context, this research provides more than a few unexpected outcomes. Personally, that's the most exciting type of research—that which uncovers surprising facts that lead to positive and practical direction for the future.

Among the many discoveries in these pages are revelations about Millennials concerning their struggle to nail down their purpose in life; the mental and emotional fragility of the generation; their appreciation for Jesus Christ and the Bible, but not for organized Christianity; and the daunting challenges they face with relationships.

Anyway, you'll read about all of this and much more. Don't miss the Afterword that I wrote to discuss, in greater detail, the outcomes that stood out to me, why they strike me as particularly meaningful, and ways in which we might reasonably respond to those opportunities for transformation.

I hope this report is as eye-opening and helpful to you as it is to me. I am indebted to Foundations of Freedom for requesting and underwriting the project, and for giving me the leeway to take the research in any direction that seemed to promise the greatest dividends for our nation. As always, the project would not have been possible without the help of my colleagues at the Cultural Research Center at Arizona Christian University.

Make the most of today,

George Barna
Director of Research
Cultural Research Center at Arizona Christian University
Professor, Arizona Christian University
Founder, The Barna Group

Introduction

Despite this being an era characterized by the presence of more information than humans can usefully process, many Americans harbor caricatures of the youngest of our nation's adult generations: the Millennials. With social media and instant punditry running amok, generating a multitude of unsubstantiated and often-conflicting opinions, analyses, and observations about the generation, such confusion and misunderstanding are to be expected. Perhaps our first clue to the burgeoning Millennial misrepresentation is that social scientists do not even agree on the age cohort that defines the generation!

But there are some facts that seem beyond controversy. For instance:

- Millennials are presently the most populous generation in American society. Depending on what birth cohort you assign to them, Millennials represent roughly one-quarter of the nation's total population, and about one-third of the adult population. If you consider Millennials to be the niche born from 1984 through 2002—as this report does—then they include about 78 million individuals.

- Their influence in the marketplace, despite their relative youth, is undeniable. They constitute close to four out of every 10 working-age Americans and about three out of every 10 registered voters. They are the prime segment of consumers in a nation built on consumption.

- Every generation is shaped by major world events that occur during the formative years of its members. For Millennials, some of the most important events have been the end of the Cold War, with the dissolution of the Soviet Union and the destruction of the Berlin Wall (1991); the Rodney King beatings and subsequent riots (1992); the public release of the Internet (1993); the mass shooting at Columbine High School (1999); the 9/11 terrorist attacks (2001); groundbreaking technology for young people, such as the iPod, Play Station, and iPhones (2001-2007); game-changing Internet apps like Facebook (2004) and Twitter (2007); the destructive fury of Hurricane Katrina (2005); the economic crisis of 2008; and the election of Barack Obama (2008).

- Millennials are significantly reshaping the brand landscape of America in response to their unique blend of needs. For instance, their lifestyle and dietary preferences have had a radical impact on brands such as Diet Pepsi (unhealthy additives), Victoria's Secret (sexual exploitation), Campbell's Soup (high sodium content), Harley Davidson (environmentally harmful machines), Tiffany (fewer marriages, luxury jewelry less appealing), and GameStop (replaced by online gaming). All of those and many other famous brands have become high-profile victims of young adult idiosyncrasies. Even shopping malls, a long-time anchor for the nation's economy, are struggling to stay afloat as consumers under 40 take their business online.

- As the youngest adult generation in the nation, they wield another type of influence: they comprise the primary parenting-age segment in the United States. More than one-third of the generation already serves as parents. But fewer Millennials than was true at the same age for people of prior generations have an interest in having children, and when they do have them, they are having fewer of them, and mothers start bearing their children at an older average age.

- This group is the most racially and ethnically diverse generation in our history. More than four out of 10 Millennials are non-white. Further, a large share (more than 40%) of Millennials is foreign born. These factors provide the impetus for their energetic drive for racial equality and reconciliation.

- Two attributes that characterize their life foundation are technology and fear. No prior generation has grown up with the breadth and pervasiveness of digital technology. And while prior generations have all experienced an array of personal threats to their well-being—including the likes of war, terrorism, droughts, racial discrimination, economic chaos, and political turbulence—perhaps no generation has emerged under as constant and wide-ranging cloud of threats as have the Millennials. In addition to the past threats—most of which remain very real challenges—there are many new forms of victimization such as cyber-bullying, digital identity theft, random school shootings, pandemics, and more. The sheer breadth of such hazards, as well as their devastating effects, has raised the daily tension level of young adults.

- The generation is redefining sexuality—their own and how to perceive and respond to the gender identity and sexual-orientation choices of others. With that have come new ideas and choices regarding marriage and family. Consequently, a social institution that used to be a safe harbor has now become a battleground.

- More Millennials have attended college and graduated from a four-year college—than any previous generation. However, because of changes in teaching methods, assessment standards, and performance expectations, there remains a healthy debate as to whether the amount of time spent in the classroom has actually produced the "best-educated" generation.

- They are more likely to seek collective action than individual exploits and heroism. Attributes like unity, community, and togetherness are pervasive elements of the Millennial consciousness and a foundational element of their vision for the future.

- The driving values of the generation are a blend of old and new—often in conflict with the values of prior generations—and are even sometimes contradictory to their own values set. Examples of this new values platform include rewriting the rules of employment by valuing achievements (rather than hours worked) and the social value of the tasks performed; preferring pets to children; and advocating tolerance while displaying little of it in their own behavior and attitudes.

- Immersed in the personal drama and conflicts facilitated by being tethered to social media, Millennials respond to authenticity and seek people whom they believe to be genuine.

- The faith alignments and activities of the generation bear only limited resemblance to those of prior generations. There are fewer self-professed Christians, as well as a large and growing mass of people who do not believe in a supernatural God (especially not the God of Israel) or the Bible as a source of unquestioned truth.

But there are still areas of the mind, heart, and soul of Millennials that have not been studied. That's where this project comes into the picture. This research was commissioned by Foundations of Freedom to understand our youngest adult generation at a deeper level. Foundations of Freedom is a peer-to-peer platform where believers in traditional American values unite, maximizing their collective influence and impact on society. The United States is a nation of faith, liberty, and virtue; Foundations of Freedom considers it the duty of all of us to restore those values to their rightful place at the forefront of American culture and society. In essence, the Foundations of Freedom mission is to restore the promise of America.

Toward that end, this research examines elements of the Millennial experience such as the lifestyle, hopes for the future, emotional and mental health, relationships, personal faith, and political attributes and perceptions of this group.

Directing the exploration process was veteran public opinion researcher George Barna, who worked with his team from the Cultural Research Center at Arizona Christian University. Having previously examined the worldview and political preferences of the generation, this project offered an opportunity to gain a broader perspective on the inner workings of the generation. To round out the perspective shared in this report, some of the previous insights gleaned by Barna and the Cultural Research Center are incorporated for consideration.

The partnership between Foundations of Freedom and the Cultural Research Center reflects a shared interest in going beyond the mere collection and reporting of information. The objective of offering this information to the public is to achieve three outcomes:

- *Education* – provide an accurate, current, and broader understanding of Millennials and their life context.

- *Motivation* – provoke readers to reconsider who Millennials are, what they need, and to identify ways in which all Americans can be supportive of the group.

- *Activation* – stimulate a commitment to interact more knowledgeably, honestly, and effectively with Millennials, while empowering them to pursue appropriate changes in personal lives, in their generation, and throughout the world they influence.

This report is divided into topical chapters based on the research findings. The final section is an Appendix that contains research details (methods and data), an introduction to some related resources, and brief introductions to the individuals and organizations behind this study. Following the research, Part II of this book features contributions by 11 national ministry and media leaders, speaking to the challenges raised by the research.

Quick Takes

*Millennials in America: New Insights
into the Generation of Growing Influence*

———————

Quick Takes

Close to one-half of young adults say they prefer socialism to capitalism.

VERY SATISFIED

Intimate Relationships & Friendships

LEAST SATISFIED

State of the Nation

Less than one-third say they are very satisfied, overall, with their life. The areas with which they are most likely to be "very satisfied" are their intimate relationships and their friendships. The area with which they are least satisfied is the state of the nation.

Politically, this generation is more likely to be liberal than conservative regarding fiscal matters, social issues, and governance. The biggest gap relates to social issues, with 40 percent self-identifying as liberal or progressive compared to just 29 percent who claim to be conservative.

Liberal/ Progressive   *Conservative*

Further, those who think of themselves as Democrats outnumber those who identify as Republicans by a two-to-one margin.

A majority of Millennials held a *positive* opinion of Jesus Christ, the United States of America, and the Bible.

THE DON'TS

A record-breaking 40 percent of young adults fit the "Don'ts" category:

People who don't know if God exists, don't care if God exists, or don't believe that He exists.

They were more likely to have a *negative* than positive impression of atheism.

Only one-third of Millennials claimed to believe in God

as the all-powerful, all-knowing, perfect and just creator of the universe who still rules the universe today.

 39% of 18-24 year olds identify as LGBTQ

Quick Takes

___

Three out of four Millennials believe that all religious faiths are of equal value.

A majority admit to often feeling

ANXIOUS
DEPRESSED
OR
FEARFUL

3 OUT OF 4 MILLENNIALS
said that they are still searching for their purpose in life.

2 OUT OF 3 YOUNG ADULTS
admitted to avoiding interaction with someone if it was likely to produce conflict.

Roughly **two-thirds** of the young adults align themselves with the Christian faith. Just over one-quarter of them said they do not associate with any religious faith.

Most Millennials reject the existence of absolute moral truth

and identify feelings, experiences, and advice from family and friends as their most trusted sources of moral guidance.

Seven out of 10 Millennials claimed that they are willing to sacrifice their life for something. The things they were most likely to die "to save, protect, or defend" were family members and their freedom. They were least likely to make that sacrifice for their country or their most cherished possessions.

MOST LIKELY

LEAST LIKELY

The personal changes most likely to be described as "extremely desirable", listed in descending order of frequency, were:

> GREATER FINANCIAL EASE OR COMFORT

> BETTER, DEEPER RELATIONSHIPS

> BETTER PHYSICAL HEALTH

> BETTER PAYING JOB

> BETTER MENTAL OR EMOTIONAL HEALTH.

The most important issues facing the nation, in descending order of importance, were identified as:

> CORONAVIRUS MANAGEMENT
> CLIMATE CHANGE
> RACIAL DISCRIMINATION
> ABORTION
> THE ECONOMY

Issues listed by less than **2 percent of Millennials** as being among the most important included:

2%

Of the nine cultural influencer categories tested, none of them were trusted by a majority to "always or almost always tell the truth or do what is right."

> INCOME INEQUALITY AND REDISTRIBUTION

> INFRASTRUCTURAL NEED

> POLICIES RELATED TO ISRAEL

> NATIONAL DEFENSE

> NATIONAL VALUES AND MORALS

> THE PARTISAN DIVIDE AND NATIONAL UNITY

> RELIGIOUS FREEDOM

> RULE OF LAW

> FEDERAL ENTITLEMENT PROGRAMS

> MEDIA STANDARDS

The most highly trusted influencers were their parents and friends.

The least trusted entities were entertainment celebrities, popular social media personalities, and elected government officials.

Lifestyle

Every new generation likes to create a signature lifestyle and philosophy that displays its uniqueness and independence. Millennials are no different. But as the reigning "young adult generation," their lives have been under the cultural microscope for a few years. The information that follows, derived from our national survey of Millennials, provides more insights into critical elements of how this generation lives.

Searching for Purpose

One of the most attention-grabbing attributes revealed in this research regarding the Millennial way of life is their widespread desire to identify a purpose for living. While much has been made of the fact that suicide rates have been climbing amid their adoption of the nihilistic notion that life is not worth the struggle, the foundation of that notion may be the absence of a clear and compelling sense of why living makes sense.

Indeed, data from the *American Worldview Inventory*[1] showed that Millennials, more than any other generation, question the very reason for living. Less than one out of five Millennials (22%) contend that life is sacred, while half of the generation (50%) argues that "life is what you make it; there is no absolute value associated with human life." In comparison, just one-third of adults from older generations—32%—hold that same view.[2]

Add the fact that three out of four Millennials (75%) admit to "searching for a sense of purpose in life" and it brings back memories of Gen X, the generation preceding them that was well-known for its inner angst and lack of direction in life. However, Gen X never reached such lofty levels of doubt about either the value of life or their personal purpose for being on the planet.

This outcome invites a comparison of how each generation handled its doubts about the value of life and their ambiguity regarding personal purpose. Gen X was known to succumb to bouts of despair and pessimism.

Millennials have taken a different, more optimistic tact: greater self-confidence, uplifting sloganeering (e.g., "be the change," "be kind," "live the life you imagine," "follow your passion, not a paycheck," "do what makes you happy," "you can make a difference," "you got this"), heightened social consciousness, and less emphasis upon economic ascendancy (with its attendant pressures).

Worth Dying For

The underlying hopefulness of the Millennials helps to explain why seven out of 10 of them (69%) believe that there are people or conditions they would sacrifice their life to preserve.

What would they be willing to die for? Slightly more than half of them (53%) said they would be willing to die to protect their family. Of the six items evaluated, family was the only thing that a majority of Millennials were willing to sacrifice their life to protect.

Four out of 10 said they would sacrifice their life in defense of their freedom. One-third claims they would go to their grave in order to protect their friends. Fewer than three out of 10 Millennials said they would sacrifice

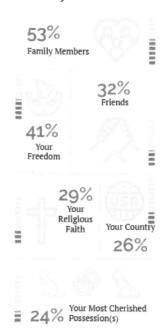

What's Definitely Worth Sacrificing Your Life For?

53%
Family Members

32%
Friends

41%
Your Freedom

29%
Your Religious Faith

Your Country
26%

24% Your Most Cherished Possession(s)

their life for their religious faith (29%), their country (26%), or their most cherished possessions (24%).

How Millennials Engage

The research briefly explored the engagement of Millennials in three dimensions of life: religious, political, and community.

About half of the generation claims to be active within the community in a typical month through either volunteering their time to a community organization or donating money to such an organization (other than a church or religious organization).

Interestingly, while half of the generation describe themselves as "deeply committed to practicing their religious faith" during a typical month, engagement in the religious behaviors tracked seems less robust. Just four out of 10 said they had attended a Christian church service or event in the past month; four out of 10 had spent at least an hour reading the Bible; and four out of 10 had donated money to a church or other religious organization.

Meanwhile, various forms of political or civic engagement showed even higher levels of participation among Millennials. About half admitted to boycotting the products or services of companies because of the organization's position on matters of importance to the individual. More than four out of 10 had engaged in persuasive dialogue with others regarding points of view related to moral, social, or political issues. One third of the group had personally participated in some type of civil protest activity —a march, rally, or demonstration that had been held during the prior month.

Life Improvements

Americans tend to believe their life can be improved. Millennials are not about to change that condition: just 5% say that their life is great and not in need of any significant changes. What kinds of changes are most highly desired by Millennials? Categorically, issues related to money and personal finances headed the list, led by a desire for greater financial ease or comfort (mentioned by 37% of the generation). Having a better-paying job (17%) and having less debt to pay off (15%) were also frequently identified as highly desirable life upgrades.

Lifestyle Activities

Forms of Civic Engagement:

 Volunteered your time to help people in your community

 Donated money to a community organization, other than a church or religious center

Forms of Religious Engagement:

 Deeply committed to practicing your religious faith

 Attended a Christian church service or worship event

 Donated money to a church, religious center, or faith-based organization

 Spent at least an hour, in total, reading from the Bible

Forms of Socio-Political Engagement:

 Avoided interacting with someone because it was likely to produce conflict

 Intentionally refused to buy a company's product or service because of their position on an issue that matters to you

 Talked to people outside of your family to try to persuade them to adopt your position on a current social, moral, or political issue

 Personally participated in a protest march, rally, or demonstration

° Activity undertaken in the respondent's past month.

As noted by other research efforts, one of the defining stresses for Millennials is excessive college debt. Between college debt payments and tax burdens, millions of Millennials have been forced to live with their parents well into their 20s and even 30s. The domino effect of that debt has been to delay marriage, childbearing, home ownership, and retirement savings, among other conditions. The overall perspective of the generation is that an increase in income might alleviate many of the pressures that have pushed the group to feel heightened levels of anxiety, and which has produced record levels of suicides and addiction.

Improvement in relationships was the category of changes next most commonly listed. Developing better, deeper relationships was a desire of nearly three out of 10 Millennials (28%). Experiencing fewer tensions related to their race, ethnicity, gender, age, or sexual orientation was listed by half as many people (13%). A similar proportion (12%) wants to be included in a community of people who know, appreciate, and respect them for who they are. About one out of 10 young adults listed having a wider circle of reliable friends as a significant desire.

Most Desirable Changes in Your Life

37% Greater financial ease/comfort

28% Better, deeper friendships

17% A better-paying job

17% Better physical health

16% Better mental and emotional health

15% Less debt to pay off

13% Few tensions with others regarding your race, ethnicity, gender, or sexual orientation

12% Inclusion in a community that knows, appreciates, and respects you

10% Higher self-esteem

10% A better relationship with your spouse/ significant other

Health and well-being were ranked third among the categories of desired changes. Having better physical health as well as better emotional and mental health were each named by one out of six Millennials as highly desirable life changes. One out of 10 listed the hope of experiencing higher self-esteem as an issue of choice.

Spiritual matters were the next most prolific category of desired changes. The biggest issue identified was having a better relationship with God (14%). Half as many identified the need to live out their faith more consistently. Other concerns in this realm included having a religious community that better met their needs and identifying a religious faith that they want to commit themselves to. Concerns about life after death were on the radar of just 2% of Millennials.

Family issues emerged as a fifth-ranked category of concerns. One out of 10 young adults said that they want a better relationship with their spouse or significant other. Other desired changes in this realm included a better relationship with their parents, better relationships with their children, and having children.

A similar number of Millennials indicated that changes in their lifestyle are on their radar.

There was no particular change in this regard that was common to a substantial percentage of respondents. The types of changes desired included moving to a different location, having a more satisfying sex life, living in better housing, experiencing more pleasing leisure activities, and having hobbies that gave them greater satisfaction.

Interestingly, the category of change that attracted the fewest Millennials was related to personal development. The big items on the wish list in this regard were having a more fulfilling career or job and gaining a more comprehensive or deeper understanding of what is happening in the world. Completing more advanced education was also an alternative desired by about one out of every 20 Millennials.

Emotional and Mental Well-Being

It would be easy to overlook one of the most significant findings of this research—the apparent need for better mental and emotional health among young adults.

Perhaps you noticed that this need was the (statistically tied) third-highest ranked desirable change listed by Millennials. Pause for a moment and think about the last time you heard a rational and compelling conversation, based on research data, no less, that identified mental health as a critical, widespread need.

To underscore the importance of that result, consider the fact that a majority of young adults (54%) admitted to "often feeling anxious, depressed, or unsafe."

We saw earlier how relationships are a point of concern for large numbers of Millennials. But do not lose sight of the fact almost two-thirds (64%) admitted that within the past month they had "avoided interacting with someone because it was likely to produce conflict." Again, the likelihood of feeling distanced from others by the inability to (effectively and positively) communicate with them is highlighted for our consideration.

Later in this report we will consider data regarding levels of trust associated with nine divergent people of influence with whom Millennials have regular contact. The statistics point out that young adults are, at best, wary of public influencers other than parents and friends. The levels of trust they have in most of the leaders they encounter from day to day are limited.

Add to these factors that nearly one-third of the Millennial cohort (30%) describes itself as LGBTQ and the finding that 39% of the youngest Millennials (18 to 24) claim to identify as LGBTQ—and you have the makings of constant emotional turbulence and relational turmoil. The proportion of young adults who identify as LGBTQ is roughly three times the proportion identified among the combined older adults of the nation. Given the moral and political implications of such an identity, that self-characterization alone raises a range of emotional challenges.

Challenges to our mental health are to be expected. After all, most adults— and especially younger adults—now believe there is no absolute moral truth. A minority accept the Bible as a true and reliable guide for determining right and wrong. Only one-third of Millennials say they choose to always respect God and other people. No wonder young adults are feeling anxious, depressed, and unsafe. Their own attitudes and those of other Americans have created an environment that cannot help but produce such feelings. Without any anchors for truth, emotions, decision-making, relational boundaries, or purpose, a sense of anomie and disconnectedness is only natural.

Although most Millennials can name a few highly desired upgrades for their life, the generation is moderately satisfied with the diverse aspects of their life. Two-thirds of them (66%) said they are satisfied with their life overall: 29% are very satisfied and a slightly higher proportion (37%) is somewhat satisfied. Not quite one-third of the generation claim to be either not too (20%) or not at all satisfied (11%).

Satisfaction with Life Elements

When the life satisfaction of Millennials is broken down into seven specific aspects of life, a majority claims to be "very satisfied" with none of those seven life dimensions, but a solid majority is either very or somewhat satisfied with six of the seven dimensions, ranging from 56% to 67%.

The highest levels of satisfaction ("very satisfied") were accorded to their interaction with people, i.e., intimate relationships (38%) and friendships (35%). The next dimensions providing the broadest degree of high satisfaction related to their spiritual life (31%), personal health (30%), and career (27%). The lowest levels of high satisfaction were awarded to their community (23%), personal finances (22%), and the state of the nation (15%).

Life Satisfaction

	Very	Somewhat	Not Too	Not At All
Your life, overall	29%	37%	20%	11%
Your personal health	30%	37%	20%	10%
Your friendships	35%	31%	17%	12%
Your spiritual life	31%	34%	19%	6%
Your intimate relationship(s)	38%	25%	15%	15%
Your community	23%	40%	20%	11%
Your career	27%	32%	20%	15%
Your personal finances	22%	34%	23%	19%
The nation	15%	28%	28%	22%

The aggregate disenchantment of Millennials with the state of the nation is exemplified in the fact that half of them (50%) are dissatisfied while just 43% expressed some degree of satisfaction. That was the only life dimension for which a larger share of the generation held a negative rather than positive perspective.

Millennials are no different. But as the reigning "young adult generation" their lives have been under the cultural microscope for a few years. The information that follows, derived from our national survey of Millennials, provides more insights into critical elements of how this generation lives.

Ideology & Politics

Because of the contentious times in which we live, more has been written about the social and political views of Millennials than anything else. They are generally described as progressive, sympathetic to the Democrat Party, highly opinionated, activist, and concerned about the future. Like most Americans, Millennials are typically more interested in domestic than international issues.

Ideological Leanings

Journalists often simplify the process of describing people's political positions by mashing all of their views into a single characterization, such as liberal or conservative. However, more detailed analysis of people's views shows that we often hold inconsistent views across issues.

In asking people to describe their political views on three axes, the statistics indicate that Millennials lean left in all three areas.

- Four out of 10 young adults say they are liberal on social issues, like abortion and same-sex marriage, while three out of 10 say they hold conservative views on those matters. Two out of 10 claimed to have views somewhere in between.

- On fiscal issues, such as taxes and government spending, about one-third (34%) have liberal views compared to slightly fewer (30%) claiming to be conservative. Nearly as many (27%) said they hold views somewhere in between.

- Regarding the size, reach, and power of government, the results were almost identical to those regarding positions on fiscal matters: 33% liberal, 30% conservative, and 28% in between.

- The outcomes also indicate that Millennials have their most intense feelings related to social issues. Four out of 10 (39%) portrayed themselves as either "very liberal" or "very conservative" on such matters. In comparison, fewer Millennials took positions on the end of the ideological spectrum regarding government (31% were either "very liberal" or "very conservative") on fiscal issues (29%). While the "extreme" positions were about evenly split between liberal and conservative for fiscal and government issues, there was a slightly larger share of Millennials leaning to "very liberal" on social issues (22% vs. 17%).

- The progressive leanings of the generation are nowhere more obvious than in regard to their feelings about socialism. Over the past five years, more than one-third of Millennials has consistently favored socialism over capitalism. However, the current research generated some of the highest support yet for socialism: 48%.

How Many Millennials Prefer Socialism to Capitalism?

2017 44%   2018 49%   2021 48%

Sources: Cultural Research Center at Arizona Christian University, 2021; American Culture & Faith Institute, 2017-2018.

Party Preference

During the frenetic, emotion-charged 2020 presidential election cycle, a large number of Millennials registered to vote for the first time. It is estimated that about three-fourths of the generation—all of whom are of age to register—are now registered. Despite the recent uptick, Millennials remain the generation least likely to be registered to vote.

Those who are registered are nearly twice as likely to align with the Democrat Party (40%) as the Republican Party (21%). Nearly as many say they are Independent of a party affiliation (18%) as say they are Republicans. (That excludes the 3% who simply stated that they have no party affiliation at all.) Perhaps most surprising, though, is that almost one out of 10 young adults (8%) claim to be Democratic Socialists, the home base of generational heroes such as Bernie Sanders and Alexandria Ocasio-Cortez. A few Millennials labeled themselves Libertarian (4%).

Regardless of their party identification, a surprisingly small proportion of Millennials describe themselves as an "American patriot." Only slightly more than half (55%) embrace that label. This fits with data from a national survey regarding patriotism in which we found that Millennials were consistently less likely than older adults to be supportive of the United States.[3] Specifically, we learned that people in the 18-to-37 age group are less likely than their elders to:

- feel proud to be an American
- believe in and obey the U.S. Constitution
- express a personal willingness to die to protect our freedoms
- accept America's enemies as their enemies
- join the military to defend the nation if called upon to do so
- consider themselves to be "extremely" or "very" patriotic

Reactions to Terminology

The fact that only a slight majority consider themselves to be patriots makes more sense in the context of the reactions of Millennials to a handful of political words and phrases.

When asked to provide their reaction to "United States of America," barely half (53%) had a positive reaction. Further, only half (50%) had a favorable reaction to the term "democracy." In both cases, the positive reactions outweighed the negative by about a 2:1 margin. But the research also revealed that a very small proportion of Millennials had a "very positive" reaction to either the "United States of America" (just 23%) or "democracy" (18%).

Positive opinions of both liberals and conservatives were even more suppressed. Overall, only about one-third had favorable impressions of either conservatives (33%) or progressives/liberals (36%). Very small percentages held a "very positive" view of conservatives (13%) or progressives/liberals (10%).

The other term explored was "socialism," which generated a positive impression among one-third of young adults (33%) and nearly as widespread of a negative impression (28%).

It is noteworthy that Millennials are more willing to express their preference of socialism to capitalism in spite of the fact that fewer of them have a positive point-of-view on socialism. As noted, a previous study found that most Americans—and Millennials, in particular—who generally express a preference for socialism do not actually know what socialism entails in practice.[4]

Reactions to Political Terminology

	Positive	Neutral	Negative
United States of America	53%	17%	26%
Democracy	50%	23%	20%
Conservatives	33%	27%	29%
Progressives/Liberals	36%	24%	29%
Socialism	33%	27%	28%

These rather uninspiring views of elements within the political sphere match the view that Millennials possess of elected government officials. Less than one out of every five Millennials (15%) said they "always or almost always" trust elected government officials to tell the truth or to do what is right, while twice as many (28%) said they "sometimes" trust such officeholders. That positioned elected officials as among the least trusted influence agents in our culture. The same ambivalent outlook toward contemporary America is reflected in the willingness of Millennials to sacrifice their life for either the good of the country (26% would "definitely" do so) or their freedom (41%).

Issues of Greatest Concern

Asked to identify the one or two issues that they consider to be the most important ones facing the United States today, six issues were named by at least 10% of Millennials. Those issues were:

24%	Managing the Coronavirus/ COVID-19 pandemic
20%	Climate change/Global warming/ Environmental care
20%	Racial/ethnic discrimination
16%	Abortion/right to life
15%	The economy – growth, jobs, taxes, trade
10%	Discrimination regarding sexual orientation or gender identity

Only three other issues were chosen by at least 5% of young adults: character of government (integrity, corruption, trustworthiness, accountability—listed by 7%); health insurance/health care (6%); crime solutions/enforcing law and order (6%).

Meanwhile, there were more than 30 other issues that were deemed to be top-two priorities by less than 5% of the generation. Some of the more un-expected items in the non-priority category included public policies related to China (4%); government spending (3%); gun policies (3%); immigration policies and programs (3%); policing (3%); public education reform (2%); income inequality and redistribution (1%); national unity (1%); and policies related to Islamic nations (1%).

Social Activism

While impressively large minorities of the Millennials are engaged in civic activity, it should be recognized that political activism is not a driving force in the lives of most members of the generation. Less than half (44%) said that in the previous month they had talked to people outside of their family to try to persuade them to adopt the respondent's position on a current social, moral, or political issue. This may well relate to the widespread tendency among Millennials of avoiding interaction that they believe will cause friction or conflict; two out of three young adults seek to avoid such exchanges.

The most common of the socio-political responses tested was intentionally refusing to buy a company's product or service because of the organization's position on an issue that matters to the Millennial. All told, nearly half (47%) admitted to engaging in such boycott activity during the past month.

Further, one out of three young adults (33%) said they had personally participated in a protest march, rally, or demonstration during the prior month. While that is well below a majority level of action, it represents an enormous number of individuals who took some physical action to display their disenchantment with some aspect of society.

Notice that the most likely forms of political engagement were those which allowed the individual to be active but not necessarily directly confrontational with a perceived opponent.

The Faith Factor

One's relationship to the Christian faith has historically been a defining factor in the lives of Americans. In a nation whose history is one of a passion for religious freedom and world-class spiritual engagement, the decline of spiritual commitment and engagement in America has been a pillar of the nation's moral and cultural decline. That downward spiral has been fortified by the dramatic reshaping of the faith domain by Millennials.

Indifference to Faith

Religious faith is not a driving force in the life of a large share of Millennials. Only half of them (52%) say they are deeply committed to their faith. Even though two-thirds of the group claims to be satisfied with their religious life, less than half of that sum (31%) describes themselves as being "very satisfied." One gets the sense that their religious satisfaction is more attributable to lowered expectations and standards than to robust spiritual fulfillment.

In fact, the ambivalence of the age group toward faith is evident in that more than one-quarter (27%) portray themselves as not associating with any religious faith or tradition. That religious indifference is further amplified by the research revealing that three-quarters (74%) of the generation believes that all religious faiths are of equal value. And when asked whether or not they would die for their faith, a mere three out of 10 (29%) claimed they would—one of the life elements they were least willing to sacrifice their life to save or protect.

Another line of inquiry examined the significant life changes Millennials would like to make. Identifying changes related to their faith or religious life was comparatively uncommon. In fact, less than one-third of Millennials included at least one faith-related change to their top life change priorities.

Easily the most pervasive religious change desired was that of developing a better relationship with God. That upgrade was listed by one out of seven Millennials (14%). But besides that improvement in their God connection, little else made the radar in relation to faith. The other changes listed were living out their faith more consistently (named by 7%); having a religious community that better meets their needs (4%); identifying a religious faith they want to commit to (4%); and developing a sense of certainty regarding what will happen to them when they die (2%).

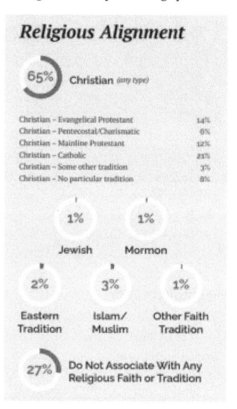

Religious Alignment

65% Christian *(any type)*

Christian – Evangelical Protestant	14%
Christian – Pentecostal/Charismatic	6%
Christian – Mainline Protestant	12%
Christian – Catholic	21%
Christian – Some other tradition	3%
Christian – No particular tradition	8%

1% Jewish

1% Mormon

2% Eastern Tradition

3% Islam/ Muslim

1% Other Faith Tradition

27% Do Not Associate With Any Religious Faith or Tradition

Christian Connection

A superficial reading of their spirituality might not suggest severe deficiencies or unsettling faith issues to address. For instance, about two-thirds of Millennials (65%) say they are Christian. That proportion is marginally less than the national average (currently 69%). Denominationally, they have similar leanings to those of older adults—perhaps a bit less likely to align with the Catholic Church, but generally presenting a similar church profile to what emerges from the nation at large.

Favorability and Trust

However, one of the most important insights from the study is that Millennials do not seem to have a problem with Jesus Christ as much as they have problems with Christian churches, Christian individuals, and some biblical principles that directly conflict with popular culture perspectives. Even the Bible fares relatively well with the group–although companion research suggests that they are ill-acquainted with its contents.

Upon asking Millennial respondents to indicate their reaction to four religious terms, the survey discovered that six out of 10 young adults (59%) maintain a positive perspective on Jesus Christ; just one out of six (16%) had a negative view of Jesus; and nearly one-fourth (23%) had no particular sentiment toward Him. For someone who has been in the global spotlight for more than two millennia, and whose life and teachings have stirred curiosity and controversy on every continent since his ministry began, that is a strikingly favorable profile awarded by a religiously turbulent population segment. But it also contains an unexpectedly large share—one out of four—who have yet to form a substantive opinion about Jesus.

Without digging too deep, though, it becomes evident that their commitment to the Christian faith is tenuous. The caution in interpreting religious activity statistics at the time the survey was conducted is that the nation was still wrestling with COVID-19 restrictions and restoration. Given that a large share of Millennials was particularly concerned about the effects of the Coronavirus, they may be a bit slower to return to prior routines than older generations, who have remained more skeptical of government claims and solutions.

Nevertheless, taking those factors into account, it seems fair to say that Millennials are currently less engaged with the Christian faith than are older adults. Exploring how many had engaged in specific faith-related activities in the past month, the survey reports that only four out of every 10 (43%) had attended a Christian church service or worship event. Similarly, just four out of 10 (40%) had spent at least an hour reading from the Bible in the past month and the same proportion (40%) had donated money to a church, religious center, or faith-based organization in the past month.

Those figures are all substantially below the national norms among older adults, which tend to be closer to six out of 10 for each of the activities evaluated. And the bar was set rather low in relation to those endeavors: attending a single church service in a month, reading the Bible for at least an hour, or donating any money at all to a religious organization.

View of Religious Concepts

In comparison, the Christian faith fared notably less well than did Jesus. In total, just half of the young adults (50%) had favorable impressions of Christianity, one-quarter (24%) had negative views, and the remaining one-fifth (19%) claimed to be neutral or undecided in their view.

The Bible placed in between those two elements, generating barely more than half (51%) espousing a positive viewpoint, slightly more than one out of five (22%) holding a negative view, and the rest (30%) not taking a position.

	Very Positive	Mostly Positive	A Little Positive	Neutral	A Little Negative	Mostly Negative	Very Negative
Jesus Christ	39%	12%	8%	17%	6%	4%	6%
The Bible	29%	12%	10%	21%	8%	5%	9%
Christianity	26%	15%	9%	19%	9%	5%	10%
Atheism	8%	7%	10%	31%	11%	8%	12%

Religious Alignment

Rounding out the list of four religious concepts was "atheism." Although there has been a precipitous rise in the number of young adults who generally fit in the "godless" camp, the concept of atheism did not sit well with the generation. Overall, only one-quarter of them (25%) held a positive view of atheism, compared to 31% who possess a negative view and the same proportion harboring a neutral stance. Overall, given that 27% of the generation admitted to not being associated with any particular faith, and that 65% of them do not endorse a biblical view of the God of Israel, the 25% favorable rating is surprisingly low.

Another way of considering those ratings is to consider the positive-to-negative ratio for each factor. In doing so we learn that Jesus Christ had a 51% vs. 16% outcome—slightly better than a 3-to-1 ratio (3:2:1). The Bible landed with a 51% vs. 22% measurement, which roughly equates to a 2¼-to-1 ratio (2:3:1). Christianity received a 50% vs. 24% rating, which was a bit lower than the Bible rating (2:1:1). Atheism got a 25% vs. 31% combination, for a negative ratio (0.8:1).

The other important reading from the favorability data is that 39% said they have a "very positive" reaction to Jesus Christ—far outdistancing the "very positive" response awarded to the other terms tested: the Bible (at 29%), Christianity (26%), and atheism (8%).

Views at the other end of the continuum are very important as well: Only 6% had a "very negative" impression of Jesus Christ, compared to 9% for the Bible, 10% for Christianity, and 12% for atheism.

It also bears mentioning that when including the five socio-political terms measured in the survey, Jesus Christ still emerged with the best rating. The 59% positive score associated with Jesus Christ bested the aggregated positive views assigned to the United States of America (53%); democracy (50%); liberals/progressives (36%); conservatives (33%); and socialism (33%).

A final consideration regarding faith imagery relates to trust in the pastors of Christian churches. Pastors were one of nine cultural influencers whose levels of trust were measured in the survey. Pastors placed in the middle of the pack.

The good news for pastors is that Millennials, on balance, are somewhat more likely to trust them than to not trust them: 54% said they would trust pastors of Christian churches to do what is right or to tell the truth at least sometimes. In comparison, 37% said they would not afford pastors even that minimal level of trust.

The more challenging news for pastors, though, is that the most important response (the "top box" response on the scale, indicating that the respondent would "always or almost always trust pastors of Christian churches to tell the truth or to do what is right") reached only 26%. Phrased differently, three out of four Millennials do not have consistent trust in the words and decisions of Christian pastors.

Using ratios again to provide comparative context, those who always or almost always trust Christian pastors outnumber those who never trust them by a 26% to 14% outcome. That is a 1.8 positive-to-negative ratio—a solid outcome, but not sufficient to suggest consistent and widespread cultural influence.

A different ratio, though, suggests that pastors may need to rethink their practices and reputation. The positive-to-negative ratio of the other eight influencers studied in the research was 1.78, notably higher than the 1.46 achieved by Christian pastors.

Millennials Have Guarded Trust Toward Christian Pastors

	Positive	Negative	Pos-Neg Ratio
Christian pastors	54%	37%	1.46
Other 8 influencers*	57%	32%	1.78

* The "other 8 influencers" were: journalists, elected government officials, college professors, their parents, entertainment celebrities, authors of non-fiction books, their friends, and popular social media personalities.

Belief Profile

While Millennials appear to have a positive reaction to Jesus Christ and even the Bible, their behavior highlights the relatively minimal effort they put in to knowing, loving, and serving Christ through biblical principles.

The Millennial survey underscored the errant views the generation possesses on some basic Christian teachings. Let's explore a few of their major religious perspectives.

God Views

- For the past decade, belief in an orthodox, biblical view of the God of Israel—that He is "the all-powerful, all-knowing, perfect, and just creator of the universe who rules that universe today"—has been on the decline.

- While *Gallup* and other surveys show that well over eight out of 10 Americans believed in God in the 1940s and 1950s, America has recently entered an era where for the first time in known U.S. history a minority of American adults believe in such a characterization of God. The *American Worldview Inventory*, the annual faith survey of Americans produced by the Cultural Research Center at Arizona Christian University, currently pegs this orthodox perspective at 46% of adults!

- Leading the parade in nouveau views of deity and divinity are Millennials. The current survey indicates that barely one-third of them (35%) possess the traditional, biblical view of God (as described above). The fastest-growing God-view comprises a segment we have labeled the Don'ts. These are people who don't know if God exists. don't care if God exists, or don't believe that God exists.

- More than four out of 10 Millennials (41%) fit this Dont's category. Notice that there are more Millennials in the Don'ts category than there are in the traditional-God definition category.

- Interestingly, the big growth in the community of Don'ts has been among those commonly perceived to be agnostics (i.e., nobody really knows if a divine being or supreme power exists). That fits with the relative indifference of this generation to faith commitment.

- The slow and virtually invisible growth of Eastern religious beliefs and practices is also evident in relation to beliefs about God. The Eastern perspective is comprised of ideas such as every human being divine (5%), or the idea that "God" simply refers to each of us reaching our full potential or a state of higher consciousness (12%). Various Eastern traditions—although they are not alone in doing so—also teach that there are many different gods or deities (8%).

- Combined, these three points of view represent one-quarter of the Millennial base. That percentage is expanding and is coming unnervingly close to the proportion that believes in the traditional, biblical view of God.

- In fitting with the "Me Generation" for which Millennials have become known, one might argue that close to one out of five Millennials (17%) have embraced a God-view that is anthropocentric. That level of human-centeredness related to God-views is unprecedented.

- Marxists, who have had such an influence on the young adult generation, have not had as much impact on God-views as they have in other dimensions of the lifestyle of this age block. Currently, only 5% argue that there is no such thing as God.

It is normal in contemporary Western society to dismiss God-view as a significant piece to the cultural puzzle. But that, of course, is part of the problem. By "canceling" God, we seek to empower ourselves and replace His authority with our own through feelings, human rationale, or expedience as viable justifications for unbiblical choices. By denying His existence we alleviate any personal responsibility to a Creator for our actions. When we replace God with people—or nothing—we become moral free agents with no higher calling, no slate of moral imperatives or guidelines, and no eternal consequences for our temporal choices.

Various Beliefs about God or A Higher Power

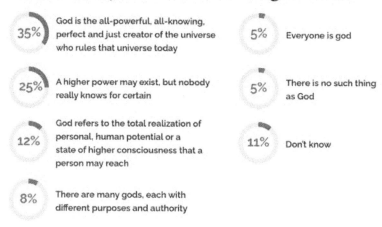

35% God is the all-powerful, all-knowing, perfect and just creator of the universe who rules that universe today

25% A higher power may exist, but nobody really knows for certain

12% God refers to the total realization of personal, human potential or a state of higher consciousness that a person may reach

8% There are many gods, each with different purposes and authority

5% Everyone is god

5% There is no such thing as God

11% Don't know

What we believe about God is foundational to who we are and how we live. That is just as true for Millennials as every other generation.

Beliefs about Eternal Destiny

Americans tend to be focused on the here and now—and each new generation over the past 70 years or so seems to be moving toward an increased preoccupation with "living in the moment."

One of the traditional emphases of Christian ministry has been understanding humans as sinners in need of a savior, and that Jesus Christ is that savior, and that salvation through Christ is a free gift offered by God to those who are willing to accept the gift on His terms.

But over the past century or so, a review of historical data suggests that Americans have become less God-dependent and more self-dependent regarding their eternal outcome.

Presently, the *American Worldview Inventory* confirms that very few Americans—just 2%—believe that they will go to Hell, or some place of eternal torment, after they die. At the same time, fewer individuals are accepting the idea that they must acknowledge their sinfulness to God and embrace Jesus Christ as their savior. In fact, a greater proportion of people now believe that they hold the key to their eternal consequences, with or without Jesus Christ being part of that equation.

The *American Worldview Inventory 2021* among Millennials revealed that a shrinking minority of the generation believes that when they die, they are certain they will go to Heaven, but only because they have confessed their sins and have accepted Jesus Christ as their savior. Whereas 28% of all adults embrace that perspective—itself a substantial decline from the 45% who adopted that belief just 15 years ago—barely half as many Millennials (16%) hold that view.

Millennials are not opposed to the idea of salvation by grace alone. In fact, when the question is posed differently than the standard measure, we found that close to half of them (46%) agreed that their eternity is based on confession of sin and acceptance of Christ—almost three times the number of young adults who said in the standard measure that Christ alone is their pathway to salvation.

Without a doubt, Millennials are struggling to make sense of both this world and the next—a struggle certainly not limited to that generation, but clearly more urgent among young adults. They inhabit a culture that rejects Christ and grace, yet they were raised at the tail end of an era when eternal security through Christ's grace was widely understood and accepted.

Which way should they go? Indisputably, they now live in the crosshairs of cultural influencers whose urgent messages about independence and self-reliance conflict with the biblical themes of Christ-dependence and personal spiritual insufficiency, resulting in widespread confusion and angst.

From an evangelistic standpoint, though, that spiritual struggle indicates that the game is not over, and the generation is not lost. Millennials simply will not be won over by outdated or unpersuasive arguments, especially when those verbal assaults are mouthed but not modeled by their contemporaries. In fact, the verbal jousting that was once the dominant mode of evangelism is unlikely to succeed with this group: they seem far more interested in observing and reflecting on real Christianity in practice.

Truth and Morality

For some time, Americans have been turning their back on the notion that absolute moral truths exist. Millennials are leading the charge. Close to six out of 10 young adults (56%) contend that "identifying moral truth is up to each individual; there are no moral absolutes that apply to everyone, all the time." The spirit of relativity has comfortably settled in among Millennials—although it should be noted that more than one-fifth of them (22%) have yet to figure out where they stand on moral truth. But among those who have taken a stand, rejecting rather than accepting moral absolutes is the dominant perspective by a 5:2 ratio (56% vs. 22%).

To those who have "ears to hear and eyes to see," it is incomprehensible that intelligent people would base moral choices on such fluid and unreliable influences as personal emotions, past experiences, and the advice of other people. Yet those are the primary inputs on which Millennials rely when making their moral decisions. Nearly two-thirds of young adults (63%) identified

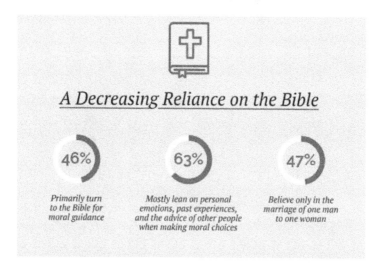

A Decreasing Reliance on the Bible

46%
Primarily turn to the Bible for moral guidance

63%
Mostly lean on personal emotions, past experiences, and the advice of other people when making moral choices

47%
Believe only in the marriage of one man to one woman

those influences as driving their moral choices while only one-fifth (19%) said they depend on a different source of moral input.

While Christians might hope that the youngest adult generation would turn to the Bible for moral guidance, a minority of the segment (46%) say that they do so. In fact, past research shows that even among people who believe that the Bible is the actual, true word of God that is a relevant and reliable guide for their life these days, many treat the scriptures as more of a back-up or emergency plan than their definitive moral guide. Once again, nearly one-quarter of Millennials (23%) have yet to land on an unwavering point of view about the role of the Bible in their moral reflections.

One example of how such perspectives become translated into real life is their views on marriage. A minority of young adults (47%) stated that they "believe in the marriage of one man to one woman because it is God's only acceptable plan for humanity, applicable to all cultures on earth." That number may be higher than many would expect, given the solid majority of Millennials that has been shown to support gay marriage and other new forms of nouveau sexual orientation and gender identification.

Worldview Considerations

As alluded to earlier, the *American Worldview Inventory* has consistently shown that Millennials are far less likely than people of other generations to possess a biblical worldview. While an estimated 9% of adults across the older pair of living generations (all of whom are now in their mid-50s or older) have a biblical worldview, that figure drops to 5% among those in Generation X and just 4% among Millennials. In fact, it drops even lower among the youngest one-third of the Millennials—namely, people in the 18-24 age niche—to a microscopic 2%!

There are several aspects of the Millennial worldview that most clearly distinguish them from their elders.[5] Let's explore a few of the dimensions in which the worldview of the youngest adult generation strays the farthest from the national norms in the areas of respect for people, civic engagement, and faith.

Respect for People

Millennials do not have as much respect for human beings as do adults from other generations.

That insight is based on a combination of beliefs and behaviors that distinguish the perspective of Millennials from that of older adults. For instance, Millennials are 15 percentage points less likely than Gen Xers to say they treat other people the same way they want to be treated; and they are 28 points less likely than Baby Boomers to embrace that approach (known to Christians as the "Golden Rule").

Millennials are also twice as likely as other people to say that the kind of people they always respect are those who hold the same religious and political views as they do. Despite their well-known advocacy of "tolerance," they emerged from the survey as the generation that is the least tolerant—by their own admission—of people who possess different views than they do.

Further, Millennials also stood out as the generation that is most likely to acknowledge that they are "committed to getting even" with those who wrong them—in fact, 28 percentage points more likely than Baby Boomers to hold a vengeful point of view.

Millennials indicated that they have less respect for life, in general. For instance, they are less than half as likely as other adults to say that life is sacred. They are twice as likely as older adults to diminish the value of human life by describing human beings as either "material substance only" or their very existence as "an illusion".

While most Americans believe that "people are basically good," that point of view conflicts with the biblical teaching that human beings are sinful and need to be forgiven for and saved from the consequences of their sins. A smaller proportion of Millennials believes that people are basically good, but their questioning of the "goodness" of humanity view is unrelated to people's sin nature. Their perspective is simply that people are not inherently valuable creatures; they are neither made in the image of God nor imbued with value due to their creation by God and being loved by Him.

America's youngest generation simply accepts the existence of humanity without assigning any spiritual or innate value to the human race. Honesty and trust are practical demonstrations of respect toward others. However, the survey also revealed that Millennials are less likely than any of the other three adult generations to claim that they keep the promises they make or to repay a loan. They are more likely than any of the other three generations to lie in order to protect their reputation or best interests.

When considered in combination, then, these findings suggest that Millennials are the generation least likely to respect other people.

Millennials are half as likely as other adults to say that life is sacred, while also twice as likely to say that the people they always respect are ones who hold the same religious/political views as they do.

Millenials are
less than

1/2   *as likely as other
adults to say that
life is sacred*

While also
being

2X   *as likely to say that the people they
always respect are ones who hold the
same religious/political views as they do*

Disengagement from Christianity

A second and more obvious distinction between Millennials and older Americans is the generation's concerns about the Christian faith. Beyond the factors described in the preceding section of this report, the *American Worldview Inventory* identifies a long list of religious distinctions between Millennials and other generations. Compared to other adults, Millennials are significantly less likely to:

- Accept the person of God as the all-knowing, all-powerful, perfect, and just creator of the universe who still rules that universe today
- Believe in the existence of absolute moral truth
- Believe that God is the basis of all truth
- Consider the Bible to be a reliable source of moral guidance
- Believe that every moral choice we make either honors or dishonors God
- Believe that human beings were created by God, in His image, but are undermined by personal sin and therefore need to be redeemed through Jesus Christ
- Believe that God loves them unconditionally
- Say they have a unique calling or purpose from God
- Accept the idea of "original sin"
- Seek to avoid sin because it breaks God's heart
- Confess their sins and embrace Jesus Christ as their savior, believed to be their only means to eternal salvation
- Accept the Bible as the inerrant word of God
- Consider themselves to be deeply committed to practicing their faith
- Pray during a typical week
- Worship or thank God during a typical week

- Study the Bible during a typical week
- Seek and pursue God's will
- Acknowledge, confess, and ask for forgiveness of their sins each week
- Believe that Satan is real and influential
- Define success as consistent obedience to God
- Believe that the universe was designed, created, and is maintained by God
- Agree that the universal purpose of humanity is to know, love, and serve God with all of our heart, mind, strength and soul

Compared to other adults—and especially Boomers and Elders—Millennials are substantially more likely to:

- Wonder if God is really involved in their life
- Believe that there is no absolute value associated with human life
- Believe that having faith matters more than which faith they have
- Consider an abortion performed to reduce personal economic or emotional discomfort to be morally acceptable
- Consider premarital sex with someone expected to be their future spouse to be morally acceptable
- Deem reincarnation to be a real possibility
- Champion liberal theology
- Be counted among the "Don'ts"—people who either do not know if God exists, do not believe that He exists, or do not care if He exists
- Contend that horoscopes provide useful guidance for their life
- Say that getting even with those who offend or harm them is defensible
- Believe that God is not involved in people's lives
- Claim that allowing people to own property facilitates economic injustice
- Karma is an undeniable, active life principle
- Conclude that the Bible is not the accurate and reliable words of God

- Believe the Bible is ambiguous in what it teaches about abortion
- Possess the idea that human beings have developed over a long period of time from less advanced life forms to our current condition

Some of the Important Theological Differences Between Millennials and Other Adults

	Millennials	Other Adults	Difference
Pray during a typical week	48%	71%	23 points
Worship or thank God during a typical week	42%	65%	23 points
Seek to avoid sinning because it breaks God's heart	42%	59%	17 points
Possess a biblical view of the nature and character of God	38%	55%	17 points
Seek and pursue God's will each week	41%	58%	17 points
Acknowledge and confess my sins each week	40%	57%	17 points
Deeply committed to practicing my faith	47%	63%	16 points
Accept the Bible as the inerrant word of God	28%	44%	16 points
Human beings were created by God, in His image	45%	59%	14 points
Have confessed my sins and embraced Jesus Christ as my savior	23%	37%	14 points
Believe God loves me unconditionally	60%	74%	14 points
Primary purpose of life: know, love, and serve God	18%	31%	13 points
God is the basis of all truth	31%	44%	13 points
Believe that Satan is real and influential	46%	59%	13 points

A New Generation Gap

The deterioration of the Christian belief and practices in American society has been in progress for more than half a century. However, the pace of that dissipation has greatly accelerated with the coming of age of the Millennials.

During their teens and 20s, Boomers also showed signs of turning their backs on the Christian faith. But they slowly morphed into a mirror image of their generational predecessors in their worldview, core religious beliefs, and most common religious practices. In fact, Boomers and Elders are surprisingly similar in their views on most of the items tested. Of the 56 questions related to religious beliefs and behavior there were statistically significant differences between the two generations regarding just 12 of the worldview factors evaluated.

In comparison, there is a somewhat wider gap between Gen X and Boomers on these matters. The generation born between Boomers and Millennials, known both as Gen X and Baby Busters, was statistically farther apart from Boomers than Boomers were from the Elders. Overall, there were 17 worldview elements for which there were statistically significant differences between Boomers and Xers.

But the faith gap between Millennials and the two earlier generations (i.e., Gen X and Baby Boomers) is the widest intergenerational difference identified at any time in the last seven decades. Statistically, Millennials are more substantially different from Gen X than Boomers had differed from the generations born immediately before or after them.

> *The faith gap between Millennials and the two earlier generations is the widest intergenerational difference identified at any time in the last seven decades.*

The largest generational gap of all is between Millennials and Boomers. (Is this where they mockingly say, "OK, Boomers"?) Of the 56 variables studied, there were significant differences related to 48 of those 56 factors between Millennials and Boomers! Further, the size of the difference between Boomers and Millennials on those items was also larger than the average magnitude of the differences between any other pair of generations.

If Not the Biblical Worldview, Then What?

The *American Worldview Inventory 2021* not only tracked the incidence of biblical worldview possession but also examined the popularity of worldviews other than the biblical worldview. Most analysts who have recognized that Americans do not have a biblical worldview have named alternatives that have lured the public. Among the options most often cited as the flavor of the day include: Postmodernism, Secular Humanism, Marxism (and its newest version, Critical Theory), Eastern Mysticism (or New Age), and Nihilism.

The overarching conclusion of the research was that most Americans have not been seduced into fully embracing any of those particular competing worldviews as much as they have simply taken bits and pieces from each of the alternative life philosophies and woven them together into a customized blend of beliefs and behaviors. That resulting worldview is known as Syncretism. The *American Worldview Inventory 2021* estimated that while only 6% of adults possess the biblical worldview—an overwhelming 88% are characterized by Syncretism.

In studying the worldviews upon which each generation is most dependent, the Cultural Research Center reached another surprising conclusion, as well. Millennials (along with Gen Xers) are considerably more likely than older generations to rely more upon Moralistic Therapeutic Deism for worldview guidance than upon any of the other worldview alternatives tested.[6]

Moralistic Therapeutic Deism (MTD) is a worldview initially identified and named by sociologists Christian Smith and Melinda Denton. They introduced their findings and conclusions in their book[7], *Soul Searching*, published in 2005 and which was based on national research among the teenagers of the turn of the millennium. In the course of their research, the two academicians identified several core beliefs that characterized the thinking and behavior of the group. Those components included:

- belief in a God who remains distant from people's lives
- people are supposed to be good to each other (i.e., moral)
- the universal purpose of life is being happy and feeling good about oneself
- there are no absolute moral truths
- God allows "good people" into Heaven
- God places very limited demands on people

Consistent with other worldview research, the current Cultural Research Center findings confirm that even though those perspectives developed two decades ago, during the preteen years of that generation (the group we now call Millennials), they have held on to those beliefs as they have aged.

That follows the well-established worldview developmental pattern. Research conducted by George Barna, and subsequently others, has shown that a person's worldview develops before they become a teenager, is refined during their teens and 20s, and then serves as a decision-making foundation for the duration of a person's life. Without intentional and consistent recasting, it is unlikely that their worldview will change significantly during a person's lifetime.

In fact, the worldview research showed that Millennials are less than half as likely to draw heavily from the biblical worldview as are adults from each of the other generations. Further, the study revealed that Millennials are less likely to rely upon the biblical worldview for guidance than from any of the six competing worldviews measured. Roughly five times as many adults in their mid-50s or older are likely to draw heavily from biblical teachings as are Millennials. Whether that is because Millennials have not had sufficient exposure to biblical teaching or because they intentionally reject those teachings is still open to speculation.

Postmodernism and Secular Humanism emerged as the other competing worldviews, besides Moralistic Therapeutic Deism, on which young adults are most likely to depend for guidance. Millennials were more likely than older Americans to lean on postmodern perspectives and behaviors.

The Worldviews Heavily Relied Upon by Generation

Percentage who rely heavily on the worldview shown	Mill	GenX	Boomers	Builders
Moralistic Therapeutic Deism	44%	38%	32%	29%
Biblical Theism (or Biblical Worldview)	9%	22%	42%	47%
Postmodernism	18%	13%	14%	17%
Secular Humanism	15%	11%	14%	19%
Eastern Mysticism	12%	7%	9%	6%
Nihilism	11%	8%	8%	13%
Marxism	10%	9%	9%	14%

Eastern Mysticism, Nihilism, and Marxism were equally likely, if not slightly more likely, than the biblical worldview to be relied upon by Millennials. Eastern Mysticism, in particular, has relative appeal to young adults: they were nearly twice as likely as older Americans to draw inspiration and guidance from Eastern philosophies and behaviors.

These Choices Have Serious Consequences

The Cultural Research Center's generational analysis of worldview preferences produced a revealing portrait of the world through the eyes of each generation. Millennials have clearly gone farther than any recent generation in cutting ties with traditional Christian views and normative biblical teaching, and have developed a very different vision of what America should become.

The research indicates that the kind of world that Millennials are seeking—and are likely to produce, as they assume greater influence in shaping our culture—would be characterized by significant changes to what currently prevails in America.[8]

1. Government with expanded reach, authority, power, and spending, in the expectation that it will facilitate a more desirable way of living.

2. Flexible and fluid public policies and programs. The syncretistic worldview that most Millennials possess means that American culture will probably become less predictable and consistent than has been the case in the past, owing to the inherently contradictory and sometimes ambiguous worldview positions adopted by young adults.

3. Episodes of violence and combativeness would be more common in a Millennial-led nation. Such conditions would be the outgrowth of various realities: a heightened degree of self-righteousness and the sense of personal sovereignty maintained by emergent adults; their dismissal of the legitimacy of institutional authority; their antipathy toward law-and-order agencies and officers; and their desire to rewrite criminal laws to reflect their more liberal worldview. The youngest adult generation is not likely to embrace one of the hallmarks of governance, i.e., progress through negotiated compromise. But they are likely to act boldly to implement their points of views given their tendency to interpret not getting their way as a personal insult or threat.

4. Political tensions will be inescapable in the short-term due to Millennials' divergent views of core perspectives related to national vision, disdain

for compromise, national moral recalibrations, and their revisionist view of U.S. history.

5. The national Christian community will become smaller in numbers, less influential, and less economically robust. Some of the more tangible and dramatic changes resulting from the reshaping of American Christianity will include fewer people and less money being designated for global Christian missions; the reduction or elimination of existing privileges received by churches, such as tax exemptions and land-use exceptions; consistent legal challenges faced by faith-based institutions, such as Christian schools and healthcare entities; the diminished presence of prayer, the Bible, and pastors in public events; and the continued reduction in the size of historically dominant Christian denominations.

6. Interpersonal relationships will be more difficult to sustain due to declining levels of trust, diminished willingness to compromise, heightened reliance on technology for communication, and disappointments produced by the lack of moral consensus.

7. The family unit will be reshaped due to fewer formal marriages, increased levels of divorce and separation, liberalized sexual morality, and the reduced appeal of raising children.

As worldview goes, so goes society. Consequently, the importance of tracking, understanding, and responding to the worldview inclinations of Millennials cannot be overestimated. Despite daily news reports positioning the tensions among Americans as predominantly political in nature, a more astute interpretation is that the differences are driven by the distinct worldviews held by important segments of our society, such as Millennials.

As our study of worldview conditions has emphasized, people do what they believe. Over the past several decades, Americans have gradually but consistently abandoned a range of foundational, biblical beliefs in favor of a consensual, emotion-driven, human-focused understanding of and response to the world.

That transition has been highly visible in relation to moral and political preferences, but it has affected every dimension of American life just as profoundly.

Millennial Connections: Examining Their Relationships

Relationships are a big deal for all of us, but they seem especially central in the minds and hearts of Millennials. But doing well in this area is perhaps more difficult for this generation than for their predecessors. While healthy and supportive relationships are certainly considered a central part of a meaningful and fulfilling life, Millennials' rearing and current cultural perspectives have made the development of positive relationships a point of hardship and frustration for millions of them.

Think about how different it is for Millennials to form deep, lasting, reliable connections compared to the relevant conditions faced by Boomers when they were of the same age.

- *Having been raised to expect the best*—and to believe they deserve it—Millennials have struggled in their quest for lasting intimate/romantic/spousal relationships. Their perceived mission is monumental: to find "the right one." This pressure has raised fears and anxieties—and sometimes depression—over their apparent inability to do so. Even the connections they do form eventually falter as they question whether there is a better relational possibility awaiting them. This "failure is not an option" mindset has plagued many young adults.

- *With more than 20 million Millennials raised in a broken family*—and virtually all of the individuals in the generation grew up close to peers who experienced divorce or other severe family dysfunction—they are understandably gun-shy about marriage. They do not want to repeat the same mistake made by the millions of divorced or unhappily married adults who preceded them. While that commitment to establishing a lasting positive relationship with a spouse is commendable, the fear of making the wrong choice is relationally paralyzing for millions of young adults.

- *Communication is an art that has been undermined*, rather than enhanced, by technology. Sociologists have confirmed that a large share of communications among Millennials takes place through their tech devices: social media, texting, phone calls, chat, etc. A growing body of research is explaining how our reliance on machines for communication greatly hinders the development of healthy interpersonal connections.

- *Financial challenges* have made marriage, in particular, difficult. Young adults, products of their culture, worry about a variety of financial considerations associated with their relationships: control, the power balance, dependency, pre-existing debt (e.g., student loans), and the insecure economics of the gig economy.

- *Issues related to sexual orientation and gender identity* were not nearly as widespread or high profile for people of prior generations. Blazing new territory, such as championing divergent identities and relationships based on innovative definitions of sexuality, has substantially increased the number of minefields scattered about in the relationship game.

- *Hovering parents*—the much-caricatured "helicopter parents"—are a reality and they continue to exert a withering degree of pressure on their children to find someone with whom they can build a future. Especially if that future will finally move the adult-child out of the parents' home.

- *The impact of being the first generation to grow up with comprehensive "Disney influence"*—i.e., you can be anything your heart desires, you can win the person of your dreams, good always defeats evil, dreams and fairy tales come true, physical beauty is the pathway to happiness, there is one right person waiting for you, and so forth—has distorted their sense of genuine relationship, caused an excessive emphasis on self, and increased the felt need to prove self-worth. (Disney, by the way, had lots of help in conveying these concepts to a culture eager to embrace such fantasies and deceptions.)

The result of all of these challenges concerning family formation has been fewer Millennials getting married; fewer having children; more having children outside of marriage; more cohabitation; marriage, when it occurs, happening later in life; an increase in pre-nuptial agreements, even among working and middle-class Millennials; and fewer faith-based weddings. The impact of such pressures on friendships has been no less dramatic, with a regularly shifting base of individuals deemed their "core relationships."

Relational Satisfaction

Compared to other aspects of their life, Millennials are prone to believe that their relationships are in good shape. About two out of three described their friendships as either very or somewhat satisfying (68%) and nearly as many claimed their intimate relationships to be similarly satisfying (63%). Note that those two types of relationships were more likely than any other dimension in their life to register as "very satisfying" (35% and 38% respectively).

Yet, the life changes they described as "extremely desirable" were more likely to relate to relationships than to any other aspect of their life in need of improvement. Close to six out of 10 Millennials mentioned a relationship change as being "extremely desirable"—and that does not count those who listed their personal relationship with God (which generated a 14% response).

The only thing that more Millennials are desperate for than better and deeper relationships was financial comfort. In total, about three out of 10 young adults said having better, deeper friendships was an "extremely desirable" change they desire. It appears that one factor hampering their relational capacity are prejudices against them based on their race, ethnicity, gender, or sexual orientation—a concern listed by 13%. A similar proportion said they desire to be part of a community that "knows, appreciates, and respects" them, a wish expressed by 12%.

Those three desires were among the top 10 listed by all Millennials. The survey also found that close to one out of 10 (9%) has an extreme desire to have a wider circle of reliable and enjoyable friends.

Family relationships weigh heavily on the minds of about one out of five Millennials. Specifically, the most desired family connections they would like to upgrade include developing a better relationship with their spouse or significant other (mentioned by 10%); growing a better relationship with their parents (7%) or their children (5%); and having children (4%). While not necessarily a relational issue, 6% also said that having a more satisfying sex life was an extremely desirable change they would like to experience.

The importance of family and friends to Millennials is demonstrated by the fact that more of them—in fact, a majority of them—said they'd be willing to give up their life for family members than for anything else. Friends didn't rate nearly as dear to their hearts, supporting the clear message that Millennials are struggling to have the quantity and quality of friendships that they want, but one-third of the generation said they'd be willing to sacrifice their life for that of their friends.

Because trust is such a vital aspect of friendship, the survey data on trusting different influencers provides additional insight into their relational condition. By far the people most trusted by Millennials are their parents: 46% said they could be trusted to tell the truth or to do what is right either always or almost always, with another 32% saying they could be trusted sometimes. The second-most trustworthy type of influence in their life was friends, for which 36% said they could always or almost always be trusted, and 40% said they were sometimes trustworthy. There were no other influence entities evaluated that generated trust levels close to that accorded to family and friends.

Some of the other trust levels awarded were either unexpected or disappointing—or both. For instance, college professors ranked third among the nine influencers tested, well above pastors. Speaking of pastors, as noted earlier in the report, they placed fourth in this line-up, with only one-quarter of young adults feeling pastors are consistently trustworthy, and one-seventh of them saying they can "never" trust Christian pastors.

How Much Millennials Trust Influencers to Tell the Truth or Do What is Right

	Always or Almost Always	Sometimes	Not Too Often	Never	Don't Know
Your parents	46%	32%	12%	6%	4%
Your friends	36%	40%	16%	4%	4%
College professors	27%	39%	18%	6%	10%
Pastors of Christian churches	26%	28%	23%	14%	9%
Authors of non-fiction books	18%	39%	22%	8%	12%
Journalists	17%	36%	28%	11%	9%
Elected government officials	15%	28%	32%	17%	8%
Popular social media personalities	15%	27%	31%	19%	8%
Entertainment celebrities	13%	27%	34%	18%	8%

What was not unexpected, though, were the lukewarm grades assigned to the bottom three entities assessed. Elected government officials, popular social media personalities, and entertainment celebrities were all described as not trustworthy by half or more of the Millennials.

A Personal Response from George Barna

Let me suggest that the readers of research studies like this one typically fall into one of three camps.

The first segment is comprised of people seeking knowledge. They read the pages of the research to glean facts that provide insight and understanding. They are less interested in acting on the research than keeping a mental catalog of the details.

The second group is the debaters. They use the research as fodder for conversations. Sometimes those exchanges are meant to clarify their own perspectives, but more often the research is a foundation for their critique of the entities examined. This group is less interested in applying the insights to correction responses than in quoting the findings in support of pet narratives.

The third faction consists of transformers: people who want to take action in response to the challenges and opportunities identified through the research. More often than not, individuals in this category and who are driven by their faith represent a body of servant-healers—people who want to put the love of God into action, serving those in need, and bringing about the spiritual healing and wholeness that might be possible through appropriate active responses.

This final section of the text is targeted to people in that third niche. These closing pages are a more subjective, personal response to the research outcomes in which I share my ideas about the most important results and what we may consider doing to provide practical assistance to Millennials.

Research that does not lead to corrective action is just an exercise in gathering information for its own sake. Who has time for that? This study represents a resource that is rich with insights into the present and future of Millennials—our emerging parents, intellectuals, powerbrokers, voters, consumers, professionals, church leaders, and more. For us to fail to strategically respond would be to squander an opportunity to serve God and His people.

> *For us to fail to strategically respond would be to squander an opportunity to serve God and His people.*

So, join me as we recap what we have discovered, consider different ways of joining together these pieces of the Millennial puzzle, and generate ideas about how to better address the felt and real needs of Millennials.

The Context

As we looked at 2022, the mood of the United States was ugly. Over the past decade-plus, the United States has become more ideologically, spiritually, politically, and morally divided. Millions of people admit to feeling that they have to tread carefully, even in the most innocuous of circumstances, from having spontaneous conversations with co-workers, to interacting with fellow parents at youth activities and events, to participating in public information meetings, or even when discussing current events in church-based small groups. Social media has done much to foment the division and to facilitate not only ideological echo chambers, but the micro-segmenting of the American people.

Since the beginning of the new millennium, America has become more tribal. We act as individuals but derive our strength and courage from the sense that we are part of one or more micro-communities that will "have our back" in the face of push-back. As Americans evaluate their social context, it has become common for them to mentally, if subconsciously, assign everyone to one or more social segments: "old, white evangelicals" and "working class, single Black mothers" are just two popular ones that come to mind. Once someone is thus labeled, we tend to treat them the same as others in that niche, but perhaps differently than those in other niches. The consequence of the loss of uniqueness and the prevalence of social labeling has hindered our ability to transcend the false boundaries that separate us.

That is the cultural milieu in which the Millennials have been raised and indoctrinated. They never asked to be coddled and overprotected by their parents. They were not born perceiving others on the basis of the cultural categories they filled. They had no intention of becoming lightning rods for social change. They are largely the product of the unaddressed dysfunctions of the generations that came before them—the generations that raised the Millennials to become who they are today.

As research projects like this one come along, it is a natural response to scour the data in order to identify the perceived shortcomings of the subject population and criticize those alleged failings. But all that does is stretch the culture gap a bit wider and harden the protective shields the cultural combatants have seized.

In this brief section I'd like to encourage you to look upon the Millennials as a generation that has inherited a cultural war zone but not the tools to bring peace to that war. I invite you to look upon our youngest adults as a group that we might be able to help navigate through the challenges in which we have immersed them. Rather than blasting them for a range of perceived inadequacies, perhaps we can support them with perspective, solutions, resources, and encouragement.

> *(Millennials) had no intention of becoming lightning rods for social change. They are largely the product of the unaddressed dysfunctions of the generations that came before them.*

Those of us who are older must recognize Millennials as part of our legacy to the world. The more we can empower our young adults to champion what matters, and to live in ways that will foster human flourishing, the more assured we can be that they will become the people God created them to be, and that this great nation can again be ground zero for realistic hope, tangible love and understanding, demonstrable compassion, creativity and innovation, and humble righteousness.

Perhaps you don't struggle with this problem, but I (and, it seems, many other American Christians) have to constantly remind myself that this life is not about me, it's all about God. My role is to know, love, and serve Him with all of my heart, mind, strength, and soul. That means doing more than talking the talk. Actively searching for ways to bless Millennials is a tremendous opportunity to be Christ-like to a fragile and desperate generation. It may be our greatest chance to contribute to the advancement of God's kingdom on earth. We are called to do everything with love and excellence, as if we are serving the Lord Himself. Investing in the well-being of Millennials is a tangible means of doing so.

But what does that look like?

The Challenges

We might start by identifying the variety of threats and challenges facing Millennials. Remember, this research was conducted only among members of the generation, so this is a glimpse inside their minds and hearts about their present condition.

One of the most alarming outcomes of the research is the prevalence of mental health issues that Millennials acknowledge. If this survey finds that 54% of the group acknowledges some degree of emotional fragility or even mental illness in themselves, it seems reasonable to believe that the number who struggle with such issues is even higher given the tendency of people to downplay their personal struggles and deficiencies. When individuals possess significant mental and emotional obstacles, they are not automatically pre-cluded from leading a productive and successful life, but doing so becomes much more taxing and daunting.

Consider the common types of mental and emotional challenges indicated by the survey respondents: fear, anxiety, depression, and emotional abandon-ment. As a father and relative whose family members have wrestled with all of those maladies, I have first-hand knowledge of the uphill climb involved in overcoming those obstacles to wellness. And it has become apparent to me that the most common suggestion—medication—may be part of the answer, but pills are often inadequate to deal with the depth of the issue.

Indeed, other personal struggles of this generation that are identified in the survey, such as low self-confidence and the fear of conflict, are frequently consequences of the underlying mental and emotional health issues.

But a number of the daunting challenges raised by Millennials have to do with their spiritual perspectives. For understandable reasons, millions of Millennials reject organized religion or have qualms about religious leaders, and especially about religious people who may prove to be hypocritical. Their experiences, observations, and assumptions regarding religion, spiritual beliefs, and faith practices have produced a turbulent spiritual experience. A historically large proportion of the generation is disengaged from spiritual teaching and practice, resulting in a paucity of knowledge, understanding, experience, and growth in this realm.

Spiritual illiteracy virtually resigns them to a superficial worldview in which they grasp at ideas and practices that provide immediate comfort rather than lasting truth and peace.

The resultant spiritual illiteracy virtually resigns them to a superficial worldview in which they grasp at ideas and practices that provide immediate comfort rather than lasting truth and peace. The moral chaos that characterizes the generation can likewise be traced to a dearth of coherent and pragmatic religious instruction abetted by the absence of mature moral reflection. The consequence is a generational moral code driven by comfort and convenience rather than truth and righteousness—and accepted because truth and righteousness are not regarded as necessary precedents, or even attainable realities.

That spiritual illiteracy has other dramatic effects as well. For instance, the widespread confusion among young adults regarding aspects of their identity—spiritual, sexual, and also related to their sense of purpose in life—is direct outgrowth of that spiritual wisdom vacuum. It seems that often young adults fill the void by creating a self-image that is built upon self-centeredness, self-reliance, and independence. That may be perceived as arrogance, but as much as anything it may also be a defense mechanism covering up their personal deficits with which they wrestle.

Another significant revelation from the research is the difficulty they face regarding meaningful, lasting relationships. Friendships are typically fluid among Millennials, a revolving door of intimates and acquaintances. The low level of trust that young adults exhibit toward people of all types and roles is facilitated by the hardships they experience in nurturing and retaining long-term, meaningful relationships. Their unwillingness, generally, to make lasting commitments hinders their associations. This has led to a widespread sense of disconnection.

Of course, their relational challenges can be traced to some of their behavioral tendencies. Their admission of intolerance and disrespect, for instance, deters the development of lasting bonds with others. Their low view of the value of human life contributes significantly to suffering a series of short-lived, unsatisfying connections.

These matters work hand-in-hand to undermine lifestyles that incorporate marriage and children.

Their reliance on technology in every dimension of life has done little to promote deeper and more permanent ties. As has been widely noted, they are the first generation to grow up with computers, mobile phones, and other high-tech devices as a ubiquitous and unquestioned part of their life. But the undeniable benefits derived from those devices also exact a cost in the quality of life that most Americans (not just Millennials) fail to consider.

All of these realities converge into what could be summarized as defining elements of the Millennial lifestyle. That pathway includes an apprehensive acceptance of materialism, a universal integration of technology, hyper-sensitivity to generational norms and attitudes, a kneejerk rejection of the traditions of prior generations, and a novel fusion of ideas into new morals and values.

The Root Issues

It would be unnecessary to seek a new set of strategies and action points if Millennials, as a generation, were generally pleased with their life trajectory—but they are not. The reasons seem obvious: the absence of a sense of purpose, meaning, and vision; emotional and mental health challenges; spiritual turbulence; relational hardships and dissatisfaction; and an expansive identity crisis.

In a situation with as many facets and complications as that facing Millennials, a simple answer is rarely imaginable, much less feasible. Yet, I am going to propose such a simple—though not simplistic or easy—solution to place our young adult generation on the path to wholeness.

It all comes down to worldview.

Your worldview is the foundation of your decision-making. Every choice you make emerges from your worldview, which serves as the filter through which you experience, observe, imagine, interpret, and respond to reality. And every one of the thousands of choices you make every day has consequences. That means worldview is at the heart of everything we are considering in relation to the well-being and development of the young-adult generation.

Given the centrality of worldview to the human experience, there can be no improvements to the life Millennials lead without addressing the fundamental role of worldview. And because worldview is developed and carried out in the competitive marketplace of beliefs and behaviors, think about the pervasive consequences for Millennials of rejecting the biblical worldview in favor of other, more popular alternatives.

Worldview and Purpose

The generation clearly struggles with purpose and meaning. Everyone needs a reason to get out of bed in the morning. The fact that three out of every four Millennials are, by their own admission, still seeking to know their life purpose is reflected in some of the unexpected, unpredictable, radical, and novel exploits of the generation. You might expect such qualms in the minds and hearts of children, or even teenagers. Something is amiss when it characterizes a large majority of people in their 20s and 30s.

Throughout the nation we find that more than one-third of adults in pre-Millennial generations (37%) have discovered their purpose and are making the most of their life. While that proportion is not as high as desirable, it does give greater hope that discovering personal purpose is achievable—and the experience of those who have done so also supports the notion that the process is worth pursuing.

Millennials have largely bought into worldviews that teach "life is about me." They contend that the purpose of life is to experience maximum happiness, often through personal accomplishments or comfort. They tend to view themselves as "basically good" people—we all are, in the Millennial estimation—and that we will derive insight and meaning in life through satisfying dialogue and voluntary acts of goodwill.

Unfortunately, that perspective leads to emptiness. Life is not about us; it's about knowing, loving, and serving a gracious, mighty, forgiving, and supportive Creator. He alone determines our purpose in life—the purpose for which He created and gifted each of us, and a life to which He calls us. We extract meaning from life by relating to and serving Him. Anything less is bound to result in frustration and despair. God, rather than us, must be at the center of our life in order to experience genuine purpose and meaning.

In fact, our obsession with happiness—perceiving it to be the height of success, the mark of a life well-lived—is one of the significant obstacles to actually being happy. God has ordained a superior alternative for us: joy. By prioritizing happiness, we—Millennials included—are missing out on the real treasure.

Happiness is an emotional state that is fleeting and circumstantial. It is dependent on our ability to facilitate that emotion, based on who we are and how we respond to situations and people. It comes and goes, sometimes unexpectedly or seemingly without reason. Even the definition of happiness is a moving target: what makes us happy today may not be enough tomorrow.

Joy, in contrast, is a lasting state of being, based on our connection with God and His principles. It is dependent upon our willingness to accept God's sovereignty over our lives, giving Him control and adopting His perspectives and purposes as our own. Joy is a more consistent state of well-being, providing a deeper sense of strength and assurance. It is the realization that things are well with your soul.

One of the realities that baffles many young adults is that joy is most efficiently derived from obedience to God. While few Millennials perceive success to be founded on obedience to His principles, my past research has revealed that those who have pursued that route—sometimes out of the sheer lack of remaining alternatives—typically discover that the obedient life is, indeed, a more fulfilling and fruitful existence. People who seek to intensely live for and with God more often experience high levels of fulfillment in life. Among the lessons they often divulge from their journey is the importance of giving rather than receiving. The data from this study confirms that most Millennials are open, if not enthusiastic, about serving others, so helping them to find their true purpose and to experience deeper meaning by blessing others has tremendous potential.

Worldview and Identity

In that framework, the identity crisis that is devastating the Millennial cohort is due to an ill-conceived perspective about self. The worldly view is that we must have faith in ourselves, as discerning individuals and free (read: unrestricted) moral agents. As such, a person receives their identity from the attributes they choose to emphasize: gender, age, race, intelligence, education, income, personal accomplishments, titles, and so forth. We tend to wrap our identity around characteristics that we believe will elevate our standing in the world. But that also means that our value will constantly change as the world shifts the attributes that it esteems, and as it re-evaluates where we stand in relation to other people. Like happiness, identity and value become moving targets.

The biblical worldview helps us to recognize that through a relationship with Jesus Christ, we are a new creation in God's eyes—one that never loses its value. When we anchor our identity to being children of the living God and a disciple of the Lord of Life, we may always stand tall in the world, regardless of its shifting values and identity targets.

Thus, the current obsession with landing on our preferred and ideal gender identity becomes a moot point. God determined our gender identity from before the time we were conceived by our parents. In fact, as creatures designed by God for purposes He ordained before time, we have no authority—much less competence—to make that choice. Our gender identity is a God-determined part of our unique personal profile that requires neither discussion nor self-determination.

This entire chapter of human history is reminiscent of a debate Abraham Lincoln had with a group of obstinate politicians in which the President displayed the folly of their reasoning. "Gentlemen, tell me this. How many legs does a dog have if you call the tail a leg?" Before they could reply, he provided the answer. "Four legs, sirs, for calling a tail a leg does not make it a leg."

Lincoln taught them a lesson about the discernment of reality. Contemporary arguments about sexual identity are founded on a similar misunderstanding. Choosing gender identity based upon the emotion of the moment is divorced from the physical realities and eternal plans established by the Creator.

We are told that God has tenderly, carefully, and purposefully crafted us according to His intentions, that He "made all the delicate, inner parts of my body and knit me together in my mother's womb." This was not random or incidental; it was part of His larger plan for us individually and for us collectively, drawn from His inexhaustible reservoir of wisdom and love, and accomplished within the larger framework of the unfolding of His plan for humanity.

Rejecting His intent and living according to our own preferences and desires is rebellious living destined to produce hardship. When it comes to human sexuality, choosing an alternative, unnatural lifestyle or identity may satisfy the momentary desires of the heart or whims of the culture but they inevitably prove to be unsatisfying choices that deny our reflection of God's own image and cause internal strife. The fact that He allows us to make those choices cannot be confused with His blessing of those choices.

Worldview and Relationships

Millennials also wrestle with numerous relational issues. That is nothing new to humankind.

But this generation may have applied a different combination of challenges to their efforts to develop and sustain meaningful relationships. Their emphasis in connecting with others seems to be placed on satisfying their personal needs rather than sharing experiences that meet the needs of both parties. They have acknowledged their intolerance of opposing ideas, a disrespect for humanity, and a willingness to respond to others on an emotional level regardless of the consequences.

But the history of relationships suggests that a different set of underlying principles foster positive relational outcomes. One of those that Millennials regard with skepticism is known as the Golden Rule—treating other people the way you want them to treat you. It is a simple but profound construct that has served humanity well since Jesus proposed it more than 2,000 years ago. The popular modern-day alternative, expecting preferred, differential treatment based on personal desire, also has a long history—of failure.

The relational challenges confronting Millennials may well be associated with another fundamental misunderstanding: the definition of love. While modern society has defined love to be a feeling, love is actually a commitment to seek the best outcomes for the other person. God demonstrated genuine love by sacrificing Jesus Christ, His own son, to die for the horrific, hurtful choices and actions of the people He created, enabling us to be reconciled to Him. As the human embodiment of true love, we see that it is characterized by sacrifice, loyalty, consistency, patience, kindness, humility, selflessness, trust, and optimism.

Some analysts have described Millennials as a tribe of narcissists; if so, their relationships are bound to be based on qualities that undermine lasting bonds with others.

It is exceedingly difficult to build positive, lasting, love-based relationships without recognizing that human life has intrinsic value.

Real love for others—that which is based on perseverance and commitment rather than feelings and circumstances—changes the essence of a relationship. Whether the relationship in question is a friendship or a more intimate connection, its chance of survival skyrockets if the foundation is love. But authentic love is a choice.

It is exceedingly difficult to build positive, lasting, love-based relationships without recognizing that human life has intrinsic value; that every human being deserves respect because they were created by God, in His likeness, for His purposes; and that tolerating divergent approaches to life is a prerequisite to seeing the lovable facets of others (without necessarily accepting those choices that are inappropriate). This and related surveys conducted by the author have identified these perspectives as being in conflict with the prevailing ethos of Millennials. Until that conflict is resolved, healthy and lasting relationships will remain an ongoing challenge to America's young adults.

Worldview and Mental Health

Research among psychologists, counselors, and psychiatrists parallels recent trends in conclusions from the pharmaceutical industry: increasing numbers of Americans are beset by anxiety, depression, and fear.

The National Institute of Mental Health reports that 21% of U.S. adults have some form of mental illness. Narrowing the scope to the younger half of the Millennial generation (i.e., ages 18 through 25), 29.4% are counted as having some type of mental disorder and 22.2% have a "serious" mental illness. Looking ahead, a shocking 49.5% of American adolescents (ages 13-18) are reported to have one or more types of mental illness, while 9.7% of them are described as experiencing "severe impairment" due to mental illness.[9] This situation amounts to a silent but life-changing crisis that is confronting—and reshaping—American society.

The mental and emotional health issues raised by this survey have enormous significance regarding the future of Millennials and the nation. While there are indisputably some physical issues that have created these complications for those struggling with mental and emotional issues, worldview certainly factors into how we address these matters.

It is likely that many young people are weighed down by anxieties resulting from their worldview. For instance, the widespread adoption of Karma as a life philosophy is bound to produce anxiety and depression; always waiting to get what you deserve is a sword of Damocles hanging over your head! Advocates of Karma contend that an impersonal spiritual force—"the universe" or other such descriptions—is responsible for the outcomes in this inevitable, self-directed cycle of cause and effect.

But the biblical antidote to Karma, of course, is the free gift of God's grace through Jesus Christ. The promise is that through a life-transforming, dedicated relationship with Jesus you do not get what you deserve, but instead receive life-giving gifts such as spiritual authority, forgiveness, eternal security, supernatural gifts and guidance, purpose, and much more as a consequence of your Christ connection.

In a world where Karma is real, man determines his own future, based on the accumulation of his choices. In a world where God rules, God determines man's future based on their relationship and the exorbitant love of our Creator.

A Silent Mental Health Crisis?

29.4%
of younger Millennials (ages 18-25) are counted as having some type of mental disorder

22.2%
of younger Millennials (ages 18-25) report a serious mental illness

49.5%
of American adolescents (ages 13-18) are reported to have one or more types of mental illness

Everyday circumstances can produce fear, particularly among those prone to bouts of anxiety and depression. Yes, some of that might be attributable to chemical imbalances that can be reduced through medication and exercise, but it is also likely that a biblical outlook on life will eliminate many of those fears and anxieties as well.

Consider a life in which there is no loving and omnipotent God looking out for you; in which there is no truth that is known, accessible, predictable, and reliable to influence your decisions and experiences; and there is nothing to hope for beyond your limited time on earth. Of course, that philosophy of despair and detachment causes anxiety, depression and fear! That's the perspective proposed by the human beings who concocted philosophies of life such as Marxism, postmodernism, secular humanism, nihilism, and other common worldviews.

The biblical worldview, in contrast, gives us the power, authority, wisdom and reason to live our life to the fullest. It is a worldview of hope, but not an unrealistic hope given the 2,000-plus years of testimonies of people just like you and me whose lives have been gloriously transformed by the presence, compassion, guidance and eternal preservation delivered through becoming a disciple of Jesus Christ and following the guidelines provided to us in the Bible. The divine Creator who gives us life and purpose loves us enough to protect us even more adeptly than any laudable father on Earth would do for his sons and daughters.

Realistically, we have to realize that none of these choices—believing in the presence and power of God, in the saving love of Christ, in the truth principles in the Bible, and so forth—will fully shield us from hardship or even persecution.

We will never have control over what goes on in our world. Yet, knowing that a sovereign God is in charge and active means that we do not need to be in control: He is there and can be trusted to take care of us in ways we cannot even fathom. That is one practical benefit of knowing God personally and loving Him: we receive His perfect love which dissolves all fear. Life is not the random series of events that millions of Millennials perceive it to be. How overwhelming life must be when that perception prevails. Thankfully, God not only has the power and will to control all things, but He also has a reason for everything that He allows to happen. That understanding can be a major stress reliever.

Worldview and Faith

Naturally, all of these misperceptions about life spring from inadequate spiritual foundation. Millions of Millennials adopt spiritual ideas that unwittingly undermine their lives. Some of those critical views include the belief that there is no objective or absolute moral truth; you can earn your salvation by doing enough good deeds or being a good enough person; there is no omniscient, all-powerful supernatural being (e.g., God); and the Bible is just another book of religious teachings written by men. Accepting these erroneous ideas is harmful to our health and well-being. Eliminating God, the Bible, truth, sin, salvation through Christ, and other fundamental realities from our daily lives is as unfortunate as removing air, water, gravity, and light from our world would be: life without them can neither be successfully lived nor explained.

How different life is when you accept and follow the ways of the Creator—not out of ignorance or group-think but with the passion of someone who has studied human history, God's principles and exhortations, and alternative ways of living and come to the conclusion that His way is best. It's not surprising; after all, He provided the guidance found in the Bible as an act of love, setting us up for success, preparing and enabling us to thrive on earth if we simply follow the parameters He sets forth.

It may be that the greatest act of faith on earth is to believe that there is not an omniscient, all-powerful, supernatural deity who is responsible for creating and sustaining the universe. As the Bible notes, there is evidence of God's existence everywhere we look: from the beauty and grandeur of nature and the marvel of humanity to the intelligent and complex design of the universe. Mathematicians and scientists have studied the probability of the Earth happening by chance or humanity arising from slime and reported the odds as being minimal, at best. Historians have examined the hundreds of biblical prophecies and recognized the likelihood of those already fulfilled having proven to be true is infinitesimally small.

How comforting it is to be able to turn to God's book of truths and discover how to live a productive, joyful, meaningful life. The personal testimonies of millions of followers of Christ throughout the last two millennia provide ample historical support for the veracity of the scriptures. But there are numerous ways of showing the reliability of the scriptures, too. All it takes is the willingness to do the homework and approach the information with an open mind.

God set us free from the pressure of having to earn His favor, realizing that while our sins separate us from Him, only a relationship with Jesus Christ could repair that breach. Thankfully, we do not have to track our good deeds or seek to prove that we are good people; all we have to do is understand the consequences of our failure to live perfectly and to rely upon the grace of God for forgiveness, acceptance, and eternal hope.

Knowing that 24 out of every 25 Millennials (yes, 96%) lack a biblical worldview is the paramount challenge facing the United States today. The most logical way to help Millennials succeed on Earth is to help them refine their worldview. Their reliance upon syncretism—i.e., the blending of disparate elements from a variety of competing worldviews into a personalized, custom philosophy of life that is unique but muddled and misguided—is detrimental to their well-being. If we can assist them in grasping baseline truths about life, then perhaps these contingent issues can be resolved efficiently and effectively. Anything short of fixing their decision-making foundation will be little more than placing a bandaid on a gaping, gushing wound.

Response to the Worldview Crisis

To address this crisis, a multi-part strategy will have to be carried out by the church at large. Some of the components of such a strategy might include the actions that follow.

- Millions of Millennials have no idea what a worldview is, whether or not they have one (they do), which worldview they possess, and so forth. One necessary action step is to increase public awareness and understanding about the basics of worldview (e.g., what it is, how it develops, why it matters, how it changes) and the numerous worldview alternatives that people, often unknowingly, are choosing from.

- Let's challenge theologically conservative churches, Bible-driven Christian schools and colleges, and people who possess a biblical worldview to intentionally, strategically, lovingly, and pragmatically educate the rest of the body of Christ on how to think and act biblically. Starting in-house—that is, with the body of Christ—makes strategic sense; if we cannot get our own house in order, we will waste our time trying to upgrade the rest of society. Remember, just 6% of adults have a biblical worldview, but the statistics are almost as disastrous among believers: just 19% of born-again Christians (not self-identified but theologically-defined born again individuals) have a biblical worldview as well.

- Although the Bible exhorts parents to embrace the primary responsibility for teaching their children biblical content, most of them don't. What would happen to the United States if parents owned that responsibility? How many lives would be changed if parents were dedicated to ensuring that their children knew biblical principles and applied them to all of the decisions they make?

- Imagine the consequences of raising up and supporting cultural leaders who will use their influence to challenge public decisions (laws, media reports, and other public pronouncements affecting society's choices) and promote a biblical approach to the situations in question. Bear in mind that with many public leaders, adopting biblical approaches do not need to be labeled "biblical solutions" since that would inflame the public more than inspire them at this point in history. But enabling them to see the wisdom of principles that are rooted in the scriptures will be more valuable than focusing on "who gets credit" for those principles.

- Believers with good intentions have thus far struggled to effectively bring biblical principles into public conversation and mainstream communications. To do so we may need to consider new ways, new language, and new ambassadors for this process. But we must also encourage our pastors to preach apologetically—that is, teaching God's word consistently and faithfully for His people.

- One series of studies I have conducted showed that conservative Christians are among the least likely adults in America to discuss major political and social issues because they do not know what the Bible teaches about the issues of the day. Such ignorance defiles the nation—and is a disgrace to our churches. But that is something we can easily fix.

- Harkening back to a fundamental research principle—you get what you measure—another valuable action step will be to introduce and promote helpful ways of assessing peoples' worldview. With that knowledge, we can then focus on ways to alter existing worldview components to equip individuals to make better choices and to have a more holistic and internally consistent philosophy of life.

Investing in Millennials and Beyond

My experience as a researcher and strategist in a variety of settings—business, non-profit, military, government, church, school, and family systems, among others—indicates that our efforts to help Millennials to grow will fail unless we genuinely care about them as individuals and demonstrate that we care in practical and tangible ways. Initially this might mean showing an appreciation of their admirable qualities (i.e., character) and individual strengths. We can confidently assume that they have heard enough about being snowflakes, slackers, narcissists, entitled, shallow, whiners, and self-centered.

What can you do today to reflect God's love for them, to compassionately and substantively bless their heart and soul? For the kinds of reasons identified in this study, Millennials are a generation in distress. Providing a loving and healing presence represents not only a biblical worldview in action but will also have a dynamic positive influence on them considering the value of living God's way.

How can you be that presence? Model a biblical worldview rather than just talking about it. Rote answers to tough questions and personal challenges won't get the job done. Rattling off memorized responses from a catechism won't impress, much less change, anyone. Consistently putting biblical principles into practice, however, will get noticed—and, most likely, considered and perhaps even imitated.

A biblical worldview starts with embracing biblical principles so that you can think like Jesus. But that's not the end game. You need to think like Jesus before you can act like Him. And that—the ability and determination to consistently live like Christ—is the endgame.

NOTES

1. The *American Worldview Inventory* is the annual faith survey of American adults conducted by Dr. George Barna and the Cultural Research Center at Arizona Christian University. Available at: www. culturalresearchcenter. com.

2. George Barna, *American Worldview Inventory 2020: A National Survey of the Worldview of American Adults*, Cultural Research Center at Arizona Christian University, 2020. Accessed at: www. culturalresearchcenter.com.

3. Barna, *Patriotism in America*, American Culture & Faith Institute, December 2017. Accessed at: https://static1.squarespace.com/static/5a3024ee90bad-e409dfa2cc7/t/5a334831ec212d3032c96ff5/1513310258806/ETTG_Barna_Patriotism+Report.pdf.

4. Barna, "Americans Favor Capitalism, Tempted by Socialism, Ill-Informed about Both," American Culture & Faith Institute, March 2018.

5. Much of the information and data contained in this section is from two reports written by George Barna for the Cultural Research Center at Arizona Christian University based on research from the *American Worldview Inventory*. Those reports are: "Millennials Have Radically Different Beliefs about Respect, Faith, and America" (Sept. 22, 2020) and "The Seismic Generational Shift in Worldview: Millennials Seek a Nation Without God, Bible and Churches" (May 12, 2021). Both of those reports, and many other reports regarding worldview and cultural transformation, can be accessed at www. culturalresearchcenter.com. The portions of text used from those reports and the data from those studies are used by permission from the Cultural Research Center and may not be reproduced without written permission from them.

6. More information about Moralistic Therapeutic Deism is contained in "Introducing America's Most Popular Worldview—Moralistic Therapeutic Deism," by George Barna, Cultural Research Center at Arizona Christian University, released April 27, 2021. That report can be accessed at www. culturalrsearchcenter.com.

7. The origin of this worldview is the landmark study described in the book *Soul Searching: The Religious and Spiritual Lines of American Teenagers*, Christian Smith and Melinda Denton (Oxford, UK: Oxford University Press, 2005).

8. Barna, *American Worldview Inventory 2021: A National Survey of the Biblical and Competing Worldviews of American Adults*, Cultural Research Center at Arizona Christian University, 2021. Accessed at: www. culturalresearchcenter. com.

9. National Institute of Mental Health. Accessed at: nimh.nih.gov/health/statistics/mentalhealth.

Part II: Other Voices

Insights and Practical Wisdom
From National Leaders and Experts

JOANNA DIAS

A Christian Formational Approach to Supporting Millennials

My client Natalie[1] was a successful 35-year-old Mexican-American woman working for a large corporation. Coming from a family of immigrants who spoke only Spanish, her family struggled to make ends meet when she was a child. She had now had a successful career for over a decade and lived comfortably on a six-figure salary.

However, this day, she sat in my office sharing that she was having what she called an "existential crisis." She found herself jaded by her work. She saw some of the most financially secure people in the world making decisions that negatively impacted the poor. She wondered why power corrupts. And with a heart to change the world, she wondered what more she could do with a world that didn't want to be changed?

Dr. JoAnna Dias has a Psy.D. in Clinical Psychology and Master of Arts in Spiritual Formation and Soul Care. A Millennial herself, Dias has done extensive work with Millennials both clinically and in church ministry. She recently founded Gracious Gift Ministries to support individuals in their pursuit toward wholeness and healing through their relationship with Jesus and others.

I believe that Natalie represents the wider Millennial narrative. As I listened, her words sounded like a Psalmist's lament: "Why do the wicked prosper?" (Psalm 73:3). And as Solomon cried, "Meaningless, meaningless, everything is meaningless!" (Ecclesiastes 3). There is an awareness of the existential groan. My job as her therapist was to invite her into this great lamentation, the cry of creation yearning for redemption. But I also felt deep sadness. While my client was wailing a song of protest, she had no awareness that anyone was there to hear her cry. She sat unaware of the One who has the power to redeem our helpless story.

This reminds me of another cynical group who had waited on a redeemer. The Israelites had trusted Moses to lead them out into the wilderness, believing they would get to the Promised Land. Over time, however, they traveled through the desert, but were not arriving at the Promised Land. They became unsettled and began to groan. They wanted the rich flavors from Egypt. Moses was taking too long talking to God on the mountain. They were thirsty. All they could see was that the redeemer's promise had fallen flat. Where was the milk and honey, for goodness' sake?

But as we know, God cared about the Israelites. They were His treasured people. His chosen possession, part of His larger story of redemption for the world (Deuteronomy 7:6). I believe that God has His eyes on Millennials—and that's where there's an invitation to remind Millennials that there is a worthy answer and a hope that can be theirs.

Living and Active Anchor

One of the greatest challenges that Millennials face is having an anchor to guide them. This was confirmed in Dr. Barna's research,[2] showing that three out of four Millennials are still searching for their purpose in life and the majority do not believe in an absolute truth.[3] So for a generation told that they can be happy but with no clear road to get there, it is confusing to pick a path. How can they guarantee the path they choose will lead to the happiness they desire? But this is also a generation taught to follow a syllabus and get good grades. How can they have a "perfect" life if they aren't given a syllabus? This juxtaposition feels terrifying for many Millennials.

But their anxieties go deeper than circumstances. Since the fall of humanity, the human condition now includes guilt and shame. We see this immediately in the responses of Adam and Eve in Genesis 3:7. In response to their shame and guilt, Adam and Eve cover their bodies and hide from the Lord. This hiding and covering is now part of the human condition. If we all paid attention to these underlying feelings constantly, each of us would be in a state of panic and/or depression all the time. And many Millennials now, more than ever, seem to be in tune with this anxiety and depression.

So, we need to answer Millennials' fears and despair with the hope that their lives have meaning in the Kingdom of God. Even in their daily, somewhat mundane lives, they can fully engage in God's story. Gordon T. Smith in his book, *Courage and Calling*, puts it this way: "In the midst of the simple ordinariness of everyday life, the work we do has the capacity to be good work that has profound worth and significance."[4] Moment by moment is an invitation to say "yes" to God. There is a firm foundation in our decision to choose Jesus.

We may be sinful, but we are so very redeemable. We were made by God (Genesis 1:26-27). And, therefore, we have been created for a purpose. Ontological anxiety is no longer something to quell, but can be reframed from an uncomfortable, unsettled angst to a vibrant, stirred awakening in our soul. The call to stay awake and alert, an open-handed willingness to say "yes" to God.

One of my favorite prayers that speaks to this question of uncertainty is by Thomas Merton:

> My Lord God, I have no idea where I am going,
> I do not see the road ahead of me.
> I cannot know for certain where it will end.
> nor do I really know myself,
> and the fact that I think I am following your will
> does not mean that I am actually doing so.
> But I believe that the desire to please you
> does in fact please you.
> And I hope I have that desire in all that I am doing.
> I hope that I will never do anything apart from that desire.
> And I know that if I do this you will lead me by the right road,
> though I may know nothing about it.
> Therefore, will I trust you always though

I may seem to be lost and in the shadow of death.
I will not fear, for you are ever with me,

and you will never leave me to face my perils alone.[5]

"The desire to please you does, in fact, please you." We serve such a gracious God. One who sees our hearts and believes good in us. God is not looking for us to meet a rubric. The only syllabus He has is the covenant that He made with us through Jesus Christ. And Jesus already met all the requirements, so we don't have to. Oh, to bathe in the goodness of Jesus!

This is why Millennials need to know their true identity in Christ. It's not solely about having a solid theological foundation, but also a knowledge of who we are in Jesus. Theology is good for grounding the mind, but only the Holy Spirit can ground the heart.

This means we pursue having a solid theological foundation of who God is and pursue connection with Him in experiential ways. There is no shortcut to relationship with God. Jeremiah 29:13 says, "You will seek me and find me, when you seek me with all your heart." Yes, we need a right understanding of who we are relating to. However, we cannot know Him completely without seeking Him with all of our hearts.

It is important to recognize that while our theology can be an anchor, it can also be a wall. We can use prayer—the place where we should be most known and loved—as a place to perform for, or even hide from God. However, as John Coe and Kyle Strobel remind us in their book *Where Prayer Becomes Real*, this isn't prayer:

> Prayer is trusting the intercession of Jesus. Prayer is trusting in the Spirit's intercessory groanings. ... This is why we cannot merely learn new prayer techniques; we have to reground ourselves in the good news of prayer. Like in our salvation, we come to prayer, with nothing but neediness, sin, and brokenness, but find grace, mercy, and steadfast love.[6]

Millennials are yearning for this. They don't want to "play church" anymore. They want to weep for the brokenness in our world with a God who weeps with them. They feel the weight of existential angst, and they want to know that hope is coming.

And we need to start with our own hearts, entering into prayer with authenticity. Our true selves standing before God in our original sin, in our ontological anxiety, and in our existential angst. It is here that we recognize that we are beholden to God. But in that place of desperation, we can cheer with delight that we are forgiven and safe. We belong to a God who loves us, sees us, and delights in us.

One way to do this is through John Coe's *Prayers of Intention*[7] (available as Appendix A at the end of this chapter). It is a daily prayer inviting the Christian believer into dialogue with God as soon as their eyes open in the morning. It is in this space that we can intend toward saying "yes" to God from the start of our day. It is meant to be done slowly, for 20 to 30 minutes. I encourage you to try this each day for a set time period and see how it begins to shape your heart.

As Augustine once said, "Our hearts are restless, until they can find rest in you."[8] God wants to be in relationship with us. This is the treasure. The arrival is the relationship. The anxiety is stirring us toward grace. The despair is calling us to hope. It is in the journey to Jesus that Millennials can find the pearl of great price, the purpose they are craving, and the anchor for their souls (Hebrews 6:19).

Relational Support and Guidance

Understanding how Millennials have developed can also provide insight into how to support Millennials. Typically, in the Western world, it is natural for us to move from having a secure place as a child in a family to finding our way as individuals in the world. For many, this means finding a life partner, pursuing financial independence, buying a house, and beginning their career.

However, this transition now occurs later in life than in prior generations. What used to be a transition from adolescence to young adulthood now has an intermediate developmental period where many Millennials went to college and did not fully take on financial, familial, and employment responsibilities until afterward.[9] The economic climate when many Millennials finished college also made it difficult for them to succeed. They were faced with the Great Recession. Many struggled for years to find jobs. They moved back in with their parents. And felt the weight of their student loans. This was demoralizing. For past generations, these setbacks may seem minor. But this generation was raised differently and therefore, they approach stress differently.

Millennials are often made fun of for being the generation that received participation trophies. But if that's true, it means that they may not have developed the resilience of what it means to be disappointed and try again. Millennials may not have developed the perseverance to fight for what they wanted in life or the character to demonstrate grace in the midst of embarrassment.

Furthermore, they were protected by helicopter parents. While there are some beautiful blessings of knowing that they can rely on a parental advocate, there are also ways that this can stunt growth that only happens in struggle. Children need to be lovingly launched into life. There is a healthy letting go that needs to happen between parents and their children. A letting go that empowers Millennials to enter into the struggle and grief within their souls in order to mature into grabbing hold of the hope of Christ.

This is where loving, supportive individuals outside of a Millennial's nuclear family can continue to support their healthy development. As humans, we are wired for relationship. Our brains are literally shaped by our primary caregivers. We have mirror neurons in our brains that help us to empathize and feel what someone else is feeling. And it is in these trusting relationships that we can offer both the love, as well as the challenge, this generation needs. Dan Allender puts it this way: "Love is the offer of a good gift that fits the circumstances, needs, and the personal variables of the one being loved."[10] Love is responsive and attuned to the needs of another. As 1 Corinthians 13 reminds us, love is "not rude" (v. 5), but "bears all things, believes all things, and hopes all things" (v.7). It's this kind of love that Millennials need in order to reduce their anxiety and depression and develop the capacity for the realities of life.[11]

Jesus offers a picture of relational, holistic love in His interaction with the woman at the well in John 4. Jesus is sitting at the city well in the heat of the day when He sends his disciples into the city for food. At this time of day, all of the women would have already gotten their water to avoid the sun. But as Jesus is sitting there, a Samaritan woman comes out to the well.

We don't know why yet, but this woman is not part of the normal rhythms of her society.

Her expectation of Jesus would have probably been that He would not have said a word to her. She was a woman after all, plus a Samaritan. But Jesus doesn't let the culture determine the way that He interacts with this woman. When He asks her for a drink, she gets a little persnickety with him. She calls out the cultural differences between them. Her self-protective walls are up. She doesn't expect anything good to come from this interaction.

> The Samaritan woman said to him, "How is it that you, a Jew, ask for a drink from me, a woman of Samaria?" (For Jews have no dealings with Samaritans.) Jesus answered her, "If you knew the gift of God, and who it is that is saying to you, 'Give me a drink,' you would have asked him, and he would have given you living water." The woman said to him, "Sir, you have nothing to draw water with, and the well is deep. Where do you get that living water? Are you greater than our father Jacob? He gave us the well and drank from it himself, as did his sons and his livestock." Jesus said to her, "Everyone who drinks of this water will be thirsty again, but whoever drinks of the water that I will give him will never be thirsty again. The water that I will give him will become in him a spring of water welling up to eternal life." The woman said to him, "Sir, give me this water, so that I will not be thirsty or have to come here to draw water. (John 4: 9-15)

Her sarcasm is dripping. It's clear she wants this man to leave her alone. If she was a Millennial, she might even think that Jesus is "mansplaining." She's clearly jaded. She thinks in His eyes she's worthless, so why is He bothering to talk with her?

But I love that Jesus isn't hindered. He doesn't view her walls as disrespect or rudeness. He sees the pain in her life. He sees her confusion. Maybe He even connects with a little girl still dwelling in her heart. And that's when He stops her in her tracks: "Jesus said to her, 'Go, call your husband, and come here.'" He gently suggests that he knows more about the depths of her heart. And when she admits that she doesn't have a husband, He continues. Even as He reveals the truth of her heart, He is kind. He simply states what is and waits to see how she will respond. "The woman answered him, 'I have no husband.' Jesus said to her, 'You are right in saying, "I have no husband"; for you have had five husbands, and the one you now have is not your husband. What you have said is true'" (John 4: 16-18).

Her response to His comment is to challenge Him and bring up their cultural differences again. And Jesus is patient with her. He answers her question. He treats her with value and worth. He doesn't get angry. There's something here for all of us when we feel like we are trying to do ministry and love another person, yet don't get the response we want. Jesus stayed engaged, kept moving toward her emotionally. He believed in the goodness of His gospel, and He rested in the work of the Holy Spirit to penetrate her heart.

He then makes the vision bigger:

> Jesus said to her, "Woman, believe me, the hour is coming when neither on this mountain nor in Jerusalem will you worship the Father. You worship what you do not know; we worship what we know, for salvation is from the Jews. But the hour is coming, and is now here, when the true worshipers will worship the Father in spirit and truth, for the Father is seeking such people to worship him. God is spirit, and those who worship him must worship in spirit and truth." (John 4: 21-24)

He shared with her that the issue at hand was so much bigger than where you worship—what matters is the One that you worship and the way that you worship Him. He speaks to her defenses and tells her that she doesn't need to have them. That God wants her worship, wants her heart most of all.

We see her begin to soften and meet Him in the conversation: "The woman said to him, 'I know that Messiah is coming (he who is called Christ). When he comes, he will tell us all things' (v. 25). And then, Jesus reveals Himself to her: "Jesus said to her, 'I who speak to you am he'" (v. 26). They come to a point in the conversation where Jesus is able to reveal His greatest mystery. Not only are her walls now down, but it's clear that after that she believes him. John 4:29 tells us that she goes into the town and tells everyone about the conversation. "Come, see a man who told me all that I ever did. Can this be the Christ?" It was through engaging with this woman that Jesus impacts her heart. He meets her where she is, without judgment, yet with attuned truthfulness, and she opens her heart to Him.

This is the way that we can reach Millennials—meeting them in their hurt, despair, and anger with words of life and love. It takes effort, patience, and hardiness. But the Holy Spirit always finishes His work. His words do not return void (Isaiah 55:11). We can trust that if we are faithful to plant His seeds in empathetic truth and sturdy love, He will continue to draw all people to Himself (John 12:32).

Holy Examples

As we engage relationally with Millennials, it is also important that we reflect to them what it means to follow Jesus. In his book, *The Master Plan of Evangelism*, Dr. Robert E. Coleman states:

> When it is all boiled down, those of us who are seeking to train people must be prepared to have them follow us, even as we follow Christ (1 Corinthians 11:1). We are the exhibit (Philippians 3:17f; 1 Thessalonians 2:7-8; 2 Timothy 1:13). They will do those things that they hear and see in us (Philippians 4:9).[12]

To allow Millennials to see us in action is dynamic theology.

In 1 Corinthians 11:1, Paul encourages his followers to observe him as well: "Be imitators of me, as I am of Christ." One way to reach Millennials is to simply do life with them. As you live and move and have your being in Christ (Acts 17:28), bring along a mentee. Are you going for a round of golf? Tending to your yard? Going on a hike? Going to see a movie? Grabbing some burgers? Serving the community? Ask a Millennial to join! Let them live life with you. Let them see how you make decisions. Let them see how you love your family. Let them see how you steward your daily life. It can be that simple.

Understandably, this might also scare you. We aren't Jesus, and we will make mistakes. But this is when it's so important to also let Millennials see you confess your sins and to reach for repair in broken relationships.[13] Let them see God's grace in your life. The sincerity in your living is what will shine God's light. It's not about being perfect, but about being God's humble servant, willing to say "yes" to Him, even when it's uncomfortable.

Hebrews 11 starts a long list of faithful friends of God, men and women whose behavior stood the test of time for their belief that God would come through for them despite the ups and downs of life. These examples lived day to day with the hope that the God who had revealed Himself to them would fulfill His promises. The writer of Hebrews is clear that many of them suffered. It was not an easy life to be a friend of God, but it was a life worth living, a hope worth hoping for.

This kind of living is what can inspire any generation to follow a God worth serving. The men and women of Hebrews 11 did not pick a political party, focus on their nuclear family, or seek solely their own personal happiness. They lived their life with the vision of hope. In fact,

> Some faced jeers and flogging, and even chains and imprisonment. They were put to death by stoning; they were sawed in two; they were killed by the sword. They went about in sheepskins and goatskins, destitute, persecuted and mistreated—the world was not worthy of them. They wandered in deserts and mountains, living in caves and in holes in the ground. (Hebrews 11: 36-38)

These men and women lived for the Kingdom of God to come. And they are people that the Bible encourages us to emulate. Again, they weren't perfect, but they persisted.

Furthermore, spiritual struggle is a part of life in the Spirit. As Dr. Barna's research notes, Millennials recognize that this life isn't fulfilling. Half of Millennials are dissatisfied with their lives and only 43% of them endorsed some level of satisfaction.[14] For a generation that had hoped to be changemakers, this is disorienting when we see that the world continues to be corrupt. For all the talk of a better future, suffering continues. This is not an entitled generation, but a grieving generation. One that is aching for a better life. C.S. Lewis said, "If I can find in myself a desire which no experience can satisfy, the most probable explanation is that I was made for another world."[15] This is the reality of Millennials.

In a safe relationship with God and others, Millennials need to be invited into a spiritual tradition of lamentation and spiritual groaning, a groaning the Holy Spirit Himself joins (Romans 8:26). One that David modeled in the Psalms. A prayer of grief and active trust that calls on the God of Victory, Jehovah

Nissi, to prevail over the evil in our world. And the research has shown that young adults who can acknowledge and embrace suffering as a part of their lives are the ones who hold onto their faith and transition into adulthood more securely.[16] The more that we can help them face and normalize this aspect of life, the better they will be able to navigate life.

So, let's live in the truth that we can't settle for less than a holy life before the Lord every day. Again, not a perfect life. But a life that is honest before the Lord. One that is willing. This is the life that Jesus led—and the one that we are called to follow. Supporting Millennials starts with each of us presenting a surrendered heart to Jesus daily and then inviting them to join us there.

Formed for the Kingdom

Jesus has cast a new vision for life. A Kingdom that is both here-and-now and yet-to-be. No matter which generation we were born in, we are called to live into this identity as Kingdom citizens and reflect this to the world. Unfortunately, we have at times confused our American, Western culture with the purity of the gospel. And it is in the Christian culture that we have created that many Millennials struggle.

When we approach the culture of the church, we should think less about preferences and more about the overarching liturgy that we are creating. By liturgy, I don't just mean order of service. I mean the larger rhythms of how the experience impacts our senses and permeates our souls. If we think *formationally*, we approach church with a question: How will my engagement here impact my soul in the long run? What will I look like in 20 years after giving myself to this way of living and worshiping?

This is why theology only goes so far in forming our souls. It is through our experience of everyday life that we are shaped, not simply by what we think.[17] Since our souls have a propensity to sin, we are going to be drawn in that direction.[18] Without intentional engagement, we will be passively shaped by whatever we engage with. It takes habitually directing our hearts toward God before we can have transformational change. The late Dallas Willard used to say that we are all being spiritually formed at all times. It simply depends on what we are giving ourselves to that determines if we are moving toward or away from God. We, as the church, want to make sure that we are engaging in a personal and corporate liturgy that shapes our hearts toward the Lord Jesus who loves us.

Think for a minute about the activities that you do on a daily basis. Maybe you exercise, talk to a spouse, go to work, or scroll on social media. What about on a weekly basis? Maybe you go to church, go shopping, or read a book. What about monthly? Maybe you visit a friend or go out for a nice dinner. What about yearly? Maybe you take a vacation or celebrate certain holidays. As you think about all of these rhythms, think about how they have been shaping you over time. What habits have you formed—both good and bad?

Now think about the Western Christian church. Many have built large sanctuaries, developed large stages with the best technology, added bookstores or coffee shops, preached God's word, held small groups. How do you think this has impacted the current culture? Both in positive and negative ways? How do you see how the church has shaped you and your expectation of what should happen when you are there (and when you aren't)? How do you think that the choices that pastors were making when Millennials were still in the nursery are impacting their current experience of church? This is a call to formational living that is systemic on every level.

I'd like to offer you the opportunity to do this thought exercise in your daily life. In Appendix B, I have provided a chart for you to track a couple of weeks of your life. I encourage you to simply fill it in for two weeks. When you are done, take 20 to 30 minutes to categorize your activities and then assign a color to each of the categories. Then color in your time blocks based on the category. Once you've done so, what do you notice? Prayerfully ask yourself and the Lord the following questions: What does this say about how you value your time? What does it say about what you give yourself to? What do you like about your time allotment? What would you change? If you lead a church or a Christian community, I encourage you to do this for your community as well. Examine what you value. How is that shaping those you lead?

Strategic formation is the only way that we will be able to change the systems around us that disillusion. And it begins with our own hearts and then moves outward. This systemic transformation has the power to change the church, and ultimately, the world. And it starts with one heart saying "yes" to God.

Conclusion

Millennials are a unique generation in many ways. They are grieving the hope offered by this world but are ripe for the hope of the Kingdom of Heaven. We have a new invitation to take ownership of the harvesting (Matthew 9:35-38). Helping Millennials to see and hold onto the hope in Christ Jesus as the anchor of their souls.

So, I offer you now this invitation:

> "Even now," declares the Lord, "return to me with all your heart, with fasting and weeping and mourning." Rend your heart and not your garments. Return to the Lord your God, for he is gracious and compassionate, slow to anger and abounding in love, and he relents from sending calamity. Who knows? He may turn and relent and leave behind a blessing—grain offerings and drink offerings for the Lord your God. (Joel 2:12-14)

God's promise still stands. Even now, we can return to God—and He will take us more deeply into His heart, into His plan, and into His Kingdom. Let's go there. And bring Millennials with us.

NOTES

1. To maintain confidentiality, any client mentioned in this chapter represents several Millennial clients that I have seen over time and identifying information has been changed.

2. The original research report by George Barna, *Millennials in America: New Insights Into the Generation of Growing Influence*, is included in its entirety as Part I of this book, pages 1-77. It is cited as: George Barna, *Millennials in America* in the contributions to this text.

3. George Barna, *Millennials in America*, 14.

4. Gordon T. Smith, *Courage and Calling: Embracing Your God-Given Potential* (Downers Grove, IL: IVP Books, 2011), 19.

5. Thomas Merton, *Thoughts in Solitude* (New York, NY: Farrar, Straus & Giroux, 1999), 79.

6. John Coe and Kyle Strobel, *Where Prayer Becomes Real: How Honesty with God Transforms Your Soul* (Grand Rapids, MI: Baker Books, 2021), 45.

7. John H. Coe, "Prayers of Intention," Institute for Spiritual Formation, Talbot School of Theology, Biola University (2013). Accessed at: https://static.biola.edu/studentlife/media/downloads/SpiDevResources/dailyprayersintention-110826pickett.pdf.

8. Augustine, *The Confessions*, 1, 1.5. (400 A.D.).

9. J.J. Arnett, "Emerging Adulthood: A Theory of Development from the Late Teens through the Twenties," *American Psychology* (22:2000), 469–480.

10. Dan B. Allender and Tremper Longman, *Bold Love* (Colorado Springs, CO: NavPress, 1992), 185.

11. See Laura A. Smit, *Loves Me, Loves Me Not: The Ethics of Unrequited Love* (Ada, MI: Baker Academic & Brazos Press, 2005).

12. Robert E. Coleman, *The Master Plan of Evangelism*, 2nd ed. (Grand Rapids, MI: Revell, 1993), 77.

13. Coleman, 78.

14. Barna, *Millennials in America*, 24.

15. C.S. Lewis, *Mere Christianity* (Columbus, NC: Granite Publishers, Inc., 2006), 136-7.

16. Kendra L. Bailey, et al., "Spirituality at a Crossroads: A Grounded Theory of Christian Emerging Adults." *Psychology of Religion and Spirituality*, 8:2 (2016), 99-109.

17. James K. A. Smith, *Desiring the Kingdom: Worship, Worldview, and Cultural Formation* (Grand Rapids, MI: Baker Academic, 2009), 50.

18. Ibid., 54.

Appendix A: Prayers of Intention

DAILY PRAYERS
FOR INTENTIONAL FORMATION
Pray without Ceasing: I Thess. 5:17

1. Prayer of Presenting Oneself as a Sacrifice (Rom. 12:1-2) 3 minutes: the spiritual discipline of daily presenting oneself to God as a living sacrifice, open to Him and His will in all things.

> **Prayer of Intention:** *"Lord, I am here, I present myself and my will to you as my act of worship. Here I am."*

This wakes me up daily to recognize the person of God and his independent will for us.

2. In receptivity to the Spirit, hear the Word of God (Heb. 4:12) 3 minutes

> **Prayer of Intention:** *"Lord, I am listening. What words from Scripture or what wisdom has your Spirit been bringing to my attention lately, that I might respond to them?"*

This keeps me listening for how the Spirit may be calling me through the Word and wisdom.

3. Prayer of Recollection (Phil. 3:7-9) 3 minutes: the spiritual discipline of reminding the self of its true identity in Christ (full pardon, full acceptance) and "Christ in me" (that I am not alone).

> **Prayer of Intention:** *"God, whatever I do today, I want to do this in you. I don't want to do this alone, in my own power or as a way to hide and cover. I don't want to find my identity in anything but Christ. I am in Christ, I am the beloved, and that is my true identity."* (Confess any idolatry of the self, seeking my salvation in some role, identity, competency apart from the love of Christ.)

This protects me from over-attaching to identities, roles, my own goodness (moralism), and making decisions from guilt and shame in some effort to atone for myself rather than re-realizing daily Christ's atonement and forgiveness.

4. Prayer of Honesty (Ps. 15:1-2, Ps. 139:23-24) 3 minutes: the spiritual discipline whereby we open to God and ourselves in what is truly going on in our heart in order for truth-telling to take place in our relationships and life in general.

> **Prayer of Intention:** *"Lord, what is going on in my heart right now with You, with others, with my life, my situations? Search me, O God, and know my heart. Open my heart to you today in truth, lest I deceive myself."* (Confess any idolatry)

This protects us from superficial obedience, from arrogance, closed heartedness, dullness of heart, etc. It opens the truth of myself to the truth of God, and his loving work in my life.

5. Prayer of Discernment (Eccles. 7:13-14, Phil. 2:12-13) 3 minutes: the spiritual discipline whereby we learn to watch what the Spirit is doing in us and not merely our work, to "consider the work of God," what His will is in all things versus ours or the devil's so that we can better cooperate with the Spirit. Here we seek wisdom on how to respond to His work that is ongoing within us.

> **Prayer of Intention:** *"Lord, what are you doing and what is it that you want me to become and do if I am to do your will?"*

Here we learn to wait on God and watch His work in and through us, that we might cooperate with it.

Appendix B: Tracking Your Liturgy

	Sunday	Monday	Tuesday	Wednesday	Thursday	Friday	Saturday
6:00-6:30a							
6:30-7:00a							
7:00-7:30a							
7:30-8:00a							
8:00-8:30a							
8:30-9:00a							
9:00-9:30a							
9:30-10:00a							
10:00-10:30a							
10:30-11:00a							
11:00-11:30a							
11:30-12:00p							
12:00-12:30p							
12:30-1:00p							
1:00-1:30p							
1:30-2:00p							
2:00-2:30p							
2:30-3:00p							
3:00-3:30p							
3:30-4:00p							
4:00-4:30p							
4:30-5:00p							
5:00-5:30p							
5:30-6:00p							
6:00-6:30p							
6:30-7:00p							
7:00-7:30p							
7:30-8:00p							
8:00-8:30p							
8:30-9:00p							
9:00-9:30p							
9:30-10:00p							

DR. CHÉ AHN

A Shaken Generation: Returning the Hearts of Millennials to Jesus

We are witnessing a generation that has been shaken to its core. Since the onset of the COVID pandemic in 2020, we have all felt this shaking, whether young or old, poor or rich. Much could be said across generational lines, but I want to direct our attention primarily to the current challenges facing Millennials and God's redemptive plan for America's youth.

Now more than ever, headlines bearing the words "mental health" are alerting us to one of this generation's greatest struggles,[1] and the latest research affirms the timeliness of this critical topic. According to Dr. George Barna's cutting-edge Millennial research, more than half of young adults (54%) admit to frequently experiencing feelings of anxiety, depression, or fear for their safety.[2] This is a major issue for Millennials—and an even larger problem for Gen Z. Dr. Barna astutely points out that the real number of Millennials struggling with fear and anxiety is likely even higher "given the tendency of people to downplay their personal struggles and deficiencies."[3] These findings

---

Ché Ahn is the senior pastor of Harvest Rock Church in Pasadena, California. He is also the president of Harvest International Ministry, a global apostolic network in over 65 nations, and the international chancellor of Wagner University.

fit into the wider mental health narrative, as levels of anxiety and depression increased by 25% *globally* during the first year of the pandemic.[4]

Another problem plaguing young Americans is a sense of aimlessness in life. Three-fourths of Millennials disclosed that they are "still searching for a sense of purpose in life."[5] Dr. Barna notes, "While much has been made of the fact that suicide rates have been climbing amid their adoption of the nihilistic notion that life is not worth the struggle, the foundation of that notion may be the absence of clear and compelling sense of why living makes sense."[6] These discoveries come at a time when the younger generation is increasingly less likely to believe in the authority of the Bible or in the core tenets of Christianity.[7] By and large, Millennials find themselves without an anchor on the seas of life. With no grounding for truth, morality, or purpose, they are left to fight an uphill battle against the many stresses of life, which appear all the more daunting during this unprecedented season of crisis.

Seasons of Great Shaking

Despite the chaos and uncertainty on the horizon, none of this has taken God by surprise. On the contrary, God in His eternal wisdom has a plan for this generation that is unfolding in remarkable ways.

Some 2,500 years ago, a man of God named Haggai prophesied about the very things we are living through today. The Word of God says in Haggai 2:7: "'I will shake all the nations; and they will come with the wealth of all nations, and I will fill this house with glory,' says the LORD of hosts." I believe this verse prophetically promises a global shaking as well as a global revival. The truth is that in modern civilization, we have only gone through two major shakings that have impacted every nation on earth.

The first of these was World War II. Between the years 1939 and 1945, virtually *all nations* were shaken by this unparalleled conflict, wherein up to 80 million people perished. Nations had no choice but to align either with the Allied Forces (the United States, Great Britain, and the Soviet Union) or the Axis Forces (Nazi Germany, Japan, and Italy). Only eight nations declared themselves neutral during WWII. Even when a country did not engage in physical warfare, the economics of the war left no corner of the world untouched.

The second global shaking of modern time is the 2020 pandemic that blind-sided every nation. Now in the third year of extreme shaking, we are facing not only the COVID crisis but the economic meltdown—with soaring inflation, outrageous gas prices, and ongoing supply chain shortages. Meanwhile, the escalating Russia-Ukraine conflict is creating a ripple effect that can be felt across the globe. Combine all of that with today's cancel culture and the radical agenda of the progressive left, and it seems like we are being assaulted on all sides.

In my 49 years of walking with the Lord, I have never experienced anything like what we are seeing today. What will be the result of all this shaking?

A Divine Wake-Up Call

In his book *The Problem of Pain*, C.S. Lewis wrote, "God whispers to us in our pleasures, speaks in our conscience, but shouts in our pain: it is His megaphone to rouse a deaf world."[8] I believe God wants to use the suffering that our nation is going through—and especially the Millennials—to turn their hearts back to Jesus Christ. For most people, when things are going great, they might say, "Who needs God?" But when you are suffering—when you are laid off, when your business declares bankruptcy due to the lockdown, when you are forced to take a vaccine or else jeopardize your career—God is shouting to you in your pain.

In this hour, God is issuing a wake-up call to the youth in America. Yes, there is tremendous fear and confusion amidst all this shaking, but the remedy is revival. That is what God is talking about when He says that He will fill His house with glory (Haggai 2:7). Prophecies in Scripture often have a number of applications, and there are different layers of interpreting the prophetic. I believe this prophecy is not just talking about the temple that Zerubbabel would build in post-exilic Jerusalem, but Haggai was prophesying to the New Covenant era where the Apostle Paul would be divinely inspired to write, "Do you not know that *you are the temple of God* and that the Spirit of God dwells in you?" (1 Corinthians 3:16). As born-again believers, we now have Christ in us, the hope of glory (Colossians 1:27).

The prophecy goes on to say in Haggai 2:9, "The latter glory of this house will be greater than the former." I believe the greatest days are ahead for the church. As Christians we are called to go from glory to glory (2 Corinthians

3:18). That is why Jesus said in Matthew 13:39 that the "harvest is at the end of the age." I believe the ultimate fulfillment of this prophecy is for the end times—*for us*—when we are going to see the greatest outpouring of God's glory. God is sovereignly allowing this generation to go through the purifying fires of intense shaking because He loves the world and He wants our nation to return to faith in Him.

Revival Begins in God's House

But we must ask the question, how does revival come? When looking at Scripture and church history, it becomes clear that repentance is crucial to revival. True historic revival begins when the church is revived by the Spirit of God.

Many Christians like to quote Joel 2:28, "It will come about after this that I will pour out My Spirit on all mankind." But what is God referring to when He says "after this"? If we go back to verses 12 and 13 of Joel 2, we will find the answer: "'Yet even now,' declares the Lord, 'Return to Me with all your heart, and with fasting, weeping and mourning; and rend your heart and not your garments.'" This passage goes on to exhort the people of God to "consecrate a fast," to pray in corporate assembly, and to weep and cry out in intercession (Joel 2:14-17).

I am firmly convinced that repentance must begin with the house of God, with God's people. 1 Peter 4:17 says, "For it is time for judgment to begin with the household of God; and if it begins with us first, what will be the outcome for those who do not obey the gospel of God?" Everything rises and falls with the Church. It is time for pastors and Christian leaders to take action.

In 2 Chronicles 7:14, a scripture that is familiar to many, the Lord promises, "If *My* people who are called by My name will humble themselves, and pray and seek My face, and turn from their wicked ways, then I will hear from heaven, and will forgive their sin and heal their land." Notice that God says, "If My people humble themselves and pray." He doesn't call out the lost in the world. He doesn't name a political party or corrupt officials. He says it starts with His people. God says revival begins with us.

Lukewarm No Longer

If we truly want to turn the hearts of Millennials back to God, our first point of action is that we need to humble ourselves and repent. According to the *Millennials in American* research, only 4% of Millennials have a biblical worldview.[9] Think about that for a moment. That means the vast majority of Millennials (24 out of 25) do not live their lives based on the truth of God's Word.

I believe this is because in the church at large, many pastors need to repent of the Laodicean syndrome of lukewarmness (Revelation 3:15-16). This is the result of the pastors themselves not having a biblical worldview or at least not preaching the whole counsel of God. I say this not to be mean—I am a pastor and I love the local church. But I also know that we have to look at ourselves as leaders and wonder, *What have we been preaching?*

In too many churches across America, we have been preaching seeker-sensitive messages instead of the Cross. We have bought the narrative that if we are nice and kind, we will grow our church, have more members, and win more souls. On one hand, the motive behind the seeker-sensitive church is going after souls, but the methodology is not biblical.

Many preachers don't want to offend their churchgoers, so they close their mouths on the controversial issues of our time. They won't speak out on the biblical definition of marriage and say that homosexuality is a sin. They won't bring up the issue of abortion, and by all means, they won't talk about politics around election time. In the end, we have become so conformed to this world that we become irrelevant. And I think Millennials are turned off by that. They can see our hypocrisy and naturally don't want anything to do with what we are preaching.

Therefore, it is absolutely crucial that we preach the truth. We must never compromise the truth of God's Word because of popular opinion in our culture. Holiness is non-negotiable. Our responsibility as pastors is to "speak the truth in love" (Ephesians 4:15). Only then will we see the body of Christ grow and mature.

We as pastors cannot afford to live lukewarm lives—now more than ever. One telling example that convicted me is when California Gov. Gavin Newsom declared the church as nonessential during the COVID lockdown. Abortion clinics, marijuana dispensaries, and even strip clubs and casinos were essential, but not the church. I realized that we (I am including myself) have had hardly any impact in California. I found myself repenting on behalf of the church and her leaders for our nonessential lukewarmness.

This begins with a renewed love for Jesus. We must love Him with all our heart, mind, soul, and strength (Mark 12:30). Just like the church in Ephesus was exhorted in Revelation 2, we must return to our first love. It is in this place of encountering the Father's love that we will experience revival and true transformation.

Restoring Families in America

Repentance and a renewed love for Jesus are necessary not only in the church but also in the home. You may have heard it said, "As the family goes, so goes the nation." I believe now more than ever before, it is imperative for us to see revival come to the family mountain of culture.

There are so many issues affecting American families today, including the devastating effects of divorce and fatherlessness. According to statistics, we are living in the most fatherless generation. For the past 15 years, on average every two out of five babies in America have been born into a single-parent home. That rate has more than doubled since the year 1980.[10] In Hebrew the word for *orphan* actually means "fatherless." In that light, we could say that most of the children being raised today are orphans.

In 2008, President Obama delivered a speech in which he painted a sobering picture of America's youth. Although I disagree with many of his policies and some of his values, I agree with what he said in this speech:

> Children who grow up without a father are five times more likely to live in poverty and commit crime; nine times more likely to drop out of schools and 20 times more likely to end up in prison. They are more likely to have behavioral problems or run away from home or become teenage parents themselves. And the foundations of our community are weaker because of it.[11]

This statement is just as valid today because it stresses the critical role that parents—and especially fathers—play in the home.

So many of these issues have led to the identity crisis that the younger generation is experiencing. It is stunning to see how many Millennials are identifying themselves as gay, bisexual, transgender, and so on. Dr. Barna's latest research found that 30% of Millennials self-identify as LGBTQ, including 39% of those between the ages of 18 and 24.[12]

While this is shocking to me, I believe it is part of the shaking that is serving as a wake-up call for the church. The world today is yearning for examples of healthy families, and it is high time that we truly embody the biblical model for family in our nation. Imagine what future generations will look like if we see families restored, marriages that last a lifetime, and fathers who are present at home to lead their children in the ways of God. All of this will help to heal the hearts of America's youth, and I believe at the same time, deal with the roots of identity confusion and transgenderism.

Returning the Hearts of Millennials

At this turning point in history, I believe that we are in a Malachi 4:5-6 season. These two verses contain a prophetic promise that changed my life—and by God's grace, they have the power to change the lives of Millennials in America:

> Behold, I am going to send you Elijah the prophet before the coming of the great and terrible day of the LORD. He will restore the hearts of the fathers to their children and the hearts of the children to their fathers, so that I will not come and smite the land with a curse.

In Malachi 4:5, God says that He will send the Prophet Elijah before the great and terrible day of the Lord. My interpretation of this scripture is that it does not refer to the literal coming of Elijah but instead the prophetic mantle of Elijah—a revival spirit—that will come twice in history. That first anointing fell upon John the Baptist (Matthew 17:10-13 and Luke 1:17). The second mantle is upon the church in the last days, when I believe there will be a key prophetic company to prepare the way of the Second Coming of Jesus.

These two verses in Malachi reveal that fathers specifically, and spiritual parents more generally, play a key role in ushering in historic revival. To see the hearts of Millennials return to Jesus, God is giving a prophetic invitation for fathers to turn their hearts toward their children first. Then children will turn their hearts toward their fathers.

We must note that the Word of God is specific: The primary responsibility is on the fathers. The outcome is either revival or a curse (the destruction of society). If we do not accept this divine invitation, we are going to have a cursed nation. And that is what we are beginning to see in the results of Dr.

Barna's outstanding research—a cursed situation in our nation. That is why Millennials so desperately need fathers and mothers who are actively seeking reconciliation as they shepherd this broken generation.

My "Malachi 4:6" Story

I have seen the promise of Malachi 4:6—*He will restore the hearts of the fathers to their children and the hearts of the children to their fathers*—coming to fruition in different stages of my own life.

As a child, I was separated from my father at the age of two. Due to visa problems, my mother, siblings, and I were unable to immigrate from Korea to the United States at the same time as my father. After reuniting with him in America when I was five years old, I hardly ever saw my father because he was working two jobs, as a pastor and a dental technician, just to keep our family afloat. When I did see him, my dad was often so stressed out. He often was dealing with anger issues, which were tied to traumatic experiences during his upbringing under the Japanese occupation in Korea as well as his time as a prisoner of war during the Korean War. Even though my upbringing was rocky in many ways, I was blessed with two incredible parents who both left behind a legacy as a great man and woman of God.

In 1994, I started to see breakthrough in the midst of the Toronto Blessing outpouring, when I repented of bitterroot judgments against my father. Two years later, I had one of the most life-changing experiences when God brought reconciliation to my relationship with my dad. During a heart-to-heart conversation, my father asked for my forgiveness for the sins that he had committed against me when I was a child. The power of a father's blessing was released as I heard my father say the words "I love you" for the first time in my life. So much healing came to my "orphaned" heart that day, and my life and ministry have never been the same!

Another way that God brought healing to my heart was through spiritual fathers. One of the four men who really impacted my life was Larry Tomczak, my first pastor in Maryland. Second, Winkie Pratney was a mentor who imparted a love for reading and revival history and gave me a solid theological foundation. Third was C. Peter Wagner, an incredible man of God who was my spiritual father and my apostle. Fourth was Jack Hayford, who helped mentor me to be a good pastor.

Raising Up Spiritual Sons and Daughters

As the years go by, I have become more and more aware of my need to pour into the next generation. One intentional way that my wife, Sue, and I do this is through our annual School of the Apostles, where we dedicate time to disciple and develop emerging apostolic leaders that we know personally. Events like these serve an important purpose. Yet mentoring should always be an organic part of our relationships with the younger generation. Sue and I have spiritual sons and daughters, both locally and globally, who we regularly invest our time in. Some of these are pastors in our church—most of whom are Millennials. We thank God for the quality of leaders that He has placed in our midst. It is incredible how teachable they are.

When my covenant brother Lou Engle and I started The Call prayer movement in 2000, we made a covenant with God that we are going to reach the next generation. Through the years, God used us to reach hundreds of thousands of young people, and I believe this came in the wake of our heart to recognize the value of legacy. Even when we are 80 years old, the next generation—Gen Z—will be the generation that we are going to target. And I think we need to have that kind of mentality and that kind of heart as we contend for revival in our homeland.

Reviving a Generation

For this urgent hour in America, we need to tap into divine strategies to bring about revival and reformation. In February 2021, God spoke to me to launch a new initiative called Revive California as 12 key apostolic leaders from different denominations gathered together, representing the government, education, business, and church mountains of culture. While this initiative began with California as its primary target, I believe it can serve as a template to reach all of America—as well as other nations—as we join forces to reach this generation.

The five-part strategy of Revive California includes: (1) mobilizing the church to establish houses of *prayer*, (2) equipping the next generation of *leaders*, (3) activating churches to reach their communities and regions through *evangelism*, (4) planting *ekklesias* (small groups) in the marketplace, homes, and churches, and (5) activating believers to bring *reformation* to the government mountain by voting and running for political office.

Each of these strategic "pillars" are action points that we can use to help bring Millennials back to Jesus. Generational strongholds will be broken through unprecedented unity in prayer. We will intentionally pour into young leaders so they maintain their passion for God and His Kingdom. Souls will be won through radical, Spirit-led evangelism, and discipleship will take place through organic church growth in all spheres of culture. Finally, we will see social transformation take place through godly reformers responding to heaven's clarion call for this momentous season in America.

All these things can be accomplished by the grace of God and by the power of His Spirit. Now is the time for action—to usher in an even greater Jesus People movement for this generation. Now is the time for historic revival among Millennials in America and for reformation to sweep across our land.

Notes

1. Adrianna Rodriguez, "Biden administration kicks off nationwide tour addressing mental health challenges from COVID pandemic," *USA Today*, March 2, 2022. Accessed at: https://www.usatoday.com/story/news/health/2022/03/02/covid-biden-administration-kicks-off-nationwide-mental-health-tour/9339924002/.

2. George Barna, *Millennials in America* (Part I of this text), 22.

3. Barna, *Millennials in America*, 62.

4. World Health Organization, "COVID-19 pandemic triggers 25% increase in prevalence of anxiety and depression worldwide," March 2, 2022. Accessed at: https://www.who.int/news/item/02-03-2022-covid-19-pandemic-triggers-25-increase-in-prevalence-of-anxiety-and-depression-worldwide.

5. Barna, *Millennials in America*, 14.

6. Ibid., 17.

7. Ibid., 36-40.

8. C.S. Lewis, *The Problem of Pain* (San Francisco: Harper San Francisco, 2001), 91.

9. Barna, *Millennials in America*, 43.

10. Frédéric Michas, "Percentage of births to unmarried women in the United States from 1980 to 2019," *Statista*, May 28, 2021. Accessed at: https://www.statista.com/statistics/276025/us-percentage-of-births-to-unmarried-women/.

11. Barack Obama, "Text of Obama's fatherhood speech," *Politico*, June 15, 2008. Accessed at: https://www.politico.com/story/2008/06/text-of-obamas-fatherhood-speech-011094.

12. Barna, *Millennials in America*, 23.

SAMUEL RODRIGUEZ

Restoring Millennials with the Agenda of the Lamb

Millennials in Crisis

Through studies we've now proven that the Millennial Generation is in a crisis due to their lack of a biblical worldview.

A full 40% don't believe in a God of any kind. Fewer than 30% believe the Bible is true. More than half don't believe in absolute truth of any kind. Only 4% have a biblical worldview.[1] It should be no surprise that Millennials are wondering what their purpose is in life, that they deal with high suicide rates, that they experience a lack of relational satisfaction, and that most of them deal with mental health issues.

How they got to this point stems from a condition that mirrors the historic moment captured in 1 Kings 18. The great prophet Elijah faced off against the ungodly King Ahab and the prophets of Baal in a moment of truth on Mount Carmel.

_____

Samuel Rodriguez is pastor of New Season, one of America's most influential mega churches, based in Sacramento, California. He also is president of the National Hispanic Christian Leadership Conference, one of the world's largest Christian organizations.

The dramatic confrontation could have been from an action movie. All the optics were there—the bad guys, the one good guy fighting the odds, a drought, an empty altar, and some not-so-innocent bystanders.

At the height of the tension, Elijah looked at the bystanders, the people of Israel, and bellowed, "How long will you waver between two opinions? If the Lord is God, follow him. But if Baal is God, follow him" (1 Kings 18:21 NIV).

What follows next is arguably one of the most tragic, emotionally disturbing verses in all Scripture. The Bible records, "The people said nothing." They said *nothing.* They were utterly silent.

How did the Millennial Generation reach its current spiritual state? They arrived here because the people of God said nothing. They got here because of complacent, comfortable, cowardly Christianity.

Church leaders and elders have sacrificed truth on the altar of political and cultural expediency. We allowed "likes" to become more important than loving God and collecting "followers" to become more important than the One we follow.

We have watched ideologies and social constructs emerge in our culture—ideologies counterintuitive to our Judeo-Christian value system, natural law, and absolute truth. Yet we said nothing from our pulpits.

That's the problem. Can it change? Absolutely yes. It can all be redeemed.

Luke wrote there is "nothing that God cannot do" (Luke 1:37 GNT). Another version tells us, "The word of God will never fail" (NLT). Yet another version reads, "With God nothing is or ever shall be impossible" (AMP). Even when the world is shaking, we belong to a kingdom that cannot be shaken (Hebrews 12:28).

Before COVID, more than 400,000 churches operated in America. We still have an incredible number of churches in America. We still have a large audience. But as of now, we're sharing a watered-down version of the gospel just to make people feel good. Our churches need to realign with Scripture, but we're giving massages when we should be calling for a chiropractor.

We know in our hearts that we drank the Kool-Aid. The church didn't want to confront cultural issues because it was politically incorrect and culturally inconvenient. May the Holy Spirit convict us so that we repent for acquiescing and conforming. He can give us the courage to rise and speak the truth with power.

As a prescription for how to move forward and impact the Millennial generation, I offer these seven propositions.

Proposition One: We must advance the Lamb's agenda, not a political agenda.

Millennials are sick and tired of the constant bickering.

Many Millennials identify, politically and culturally, as independents. They conflate religious affiliation, denomination affiliation, even in an evangelical worldview, with a specific political ideology. We need to clearly communicate to Millennials, "Forget about the agenda of the donkey and the elephant; here's the Lamb's agenda."

The Lamb's agenda is the prescription for personal salvation and societal transformation. The biggest battle is not between the donkey and the elephant. The biggest battle is between the Lamb and the serpent, and praise God, the Lamb already won (Colossians 2:15).

Proposition Two: We must start preaching according to the Lamb's agenda.

The best and greatest news Millennials or any generation has ever and will ever hear comes from what John the Baptist shouted 2,000 years ago when he saw Jesus walking toward him: "Behold, the Lamb of God who takes away the sin of the world" (John 1:29).

Without a strong foundation, people get lost. Knowing Jesus establishes a foundation for freedom from confusion, and free people can do what others cannot do.

- A free man approached Pharaoh in Egypt and said, "Let my people go."
- A free man stepped into the Promised Land and declared, "As for me and my house, we shall serve the Lord."
- A free man stared down a giant called Goliath and said, "You come against me with a sword and spear, but I come against you in the name of the Lord God Almighty."

- Free young men refused to bow and exhibited freedom even in a fiery furnace.

- A free man prayed down fire from Heaven, then dared to say, "Get ready, here comes the rain."

- Free men declared, "We hold these truths to be self-evident, that all men are created equal, endowed by their Creator with certain unalienable rights and among these are life, liberty, and the pursuit of happiness."

- Free men confronted the evil of slavery, then declared, "With malice towards none, and charity towards all."

- A free young man had a dream that we would live in a nation where we would be judged not "by the color of our skin but rather by the content of our character."

The most significant expression of freedom came when Christ, a free man who was Freedom incarnate, hung on a tree as a sacrifice and personified what He had declared: "For he who the Son sets free is free indeed" (John 8:36).

Jesus gives eternal freedom, freedom of the spirit. Freedom to go beyond existence into living does not come from institutions made by man.

Our freedom comes from the One who wrote the law with one finger and grace with both hands. Our freedom comes from His statement, "And you will know the truth and the truth will set you free" (John 8:32). Our freedom is based on His message, "I am the Way, the Truth and the Life. No one can come to the Father, except through me" (John 14:6).

So, what's the great news for Millennials? The great news is that through Jesus Christ, their generation can be free from a life of sin (Revelation 1:6), free from the torment of fear (2 Timothy 1:7), and free from the sentence of eternal condemnation (Romans 8:1). And when they accept Christ's freedom, their lives will never be the same.

Millennials who accept the great news will be baptized with Christ (Romans), crucified with Christ (Galatians), seated with Christ (Ephesians), strengthened by Christ (Philippians), hidden in Christ (Colossians), and reign with Him forever (Revelation).

This is the result when we declare, "Behold the Lamb of God."

Proposition Three: We must reconcile the Christian message's vertical and horizontal planes.

Our message needs to flip if we are to reach the Millennial Generation effectively. We have to offer the truth at every Sunday service, on every post, in all Bible teachings, throughout all Christian colleges and universities.

No other symbol incorporates passion and promise like the Cross. It is a simple symbol depicting two pieces of wood, one vertical and the other horizontal, that successfully branded the eternal hope of glory for all mankind.

Madison Avenue and multimillion-dollar campaigns have not been able to reproduce the loyalty, commitment, and multigenerational allegiance like the one conveyed via the humble Cross.

Like the Cross, life is both vertical and horizontal. Vertically, we stand connected to God, His Kingdom, eternal life, spiritual truths, and divine principles. Horizontally, we connect with community, family, culture, and society.

Being both vertical and horizontal, the Cross is both redemption and relationship, holiness and humility, covenant and community, kingdom and society, conviction and compassion, truth and love, righteousness and justice, salvation and transformation, ethos and pathos, orthodoxy and orthopraxy, John 3:16's faith and Matthew 25's action, sanctification, and service.

To a great degree, the Cross is the meeting place of Billy Graham's message of salvation exclusively through Jesus Christ and Dr. Martin Luther King, Jr.'s march for justice.

Millennials need to hear and see in action the Psalmist's words, "Righteousness and justice are the foundation of your throne, truth and love lead the way as attendants" (Psalm 89:14).

The rubric for engaging the next generation is righteousness, justice, truth, and love.

Proposition Four: We must embrace who we truly are.

We need to settle our own identity and purpose if we are to solve these issues for the next generation.

Who are we? Are we just another institution in society? Are we another religious faith narrative competing in the marketplace of ideas? Are we simply a feel-good apparatus for the spiritually impaired? Are we an outdated conduit for a set of irrelevant values in the world of TikTok, Twitter, or Instagram?

Who are we? When we accept and embrace that we are recipients of the best news of all, we can respond with clarity, conviction, and courage.

We are the light of the world. We are a city on a hill. We are people of the Word. We are salt and light. We are disciples, witnesses, and Christ-followers. We are evangelists, pastors, and teachers.

We are children of the Cross, witnesses of the empty tomb, and products of the upper room.

We are the redeemed of the Lord. We are the sheep of his pasture. We are forgiven. We are free and favored. We are called and chosen. We are worshipers. We are world changers and history makers.

With great deference to the beautiful tapestry of our diversity, we are not even first and foremost, Black, White, Asian, Hispanic, American Indian, or Pacific Islander. We are born-again, blood-washed children of the living God.

We are the church of Jesus Christ, and hell's gates *shall not prevail* against us (Matthew 16:18).

We are those for whom Jesus, the Lamb of God, came to equip with great news and the power to overcome. We are those who have defeated the enemy by the blood of the Lamb and by the word of our testimony (Revelation 12:11).

Most of us have overcome adversity, a storm, or a difficult chapter. We've all been through something. Some of us have been through so many storms that the National Hurricane Weather Center shows up if we Google our name.

When Jesus Christ the Lamb of God equipped us with the power to overcome those storms, we became card-carrying members of the "Overcomers Club," with the slogan, "No weapon formed against me shall prosper" (Isaiah 54:17).

As overcomers, we've learned that sometimes we have to go *through* the battle to get to the blessing. Joseph went *through* the pain to get to the palace. The Israelites went *through* the desert to get to the promised land. The Hebrew boys went *through* the fire to get to the king's court.

We have proven through storms of adversity the words, "In all these things, we are more than conquerors through Him who loves us" (Romans 8:37).

As card-carrying members of the Overcomers Club, we have the right and the authority to answer the questions of Millennials. "Why should I hope when I'm struggling so much?" "How do I cope when people are against me?" "What happens when I die?"

There is a biblical answer for every shade of a Millennial's darkness. When light stands next to darkness, light always wins. For every Pharaoh, there is a Moses. For every Goliath, there is a David. For every Nebuchadnezzar, there is a Daniel. For every Jezebel, there is an Elijah. For every Herod, there is a Jesus. And for every devil that comes against you, there is a God who is even mightier that fights on your behalf.

The reality of the gospel for Millennials is that God's purpose *is greater than the brokenness of man.*

Who are we? We are recipients of the greatest news of all time, called by His name and born for this hour. We were not born to fail. We were not born only to survive. We were born to have a life and live abundantly, and to communicate it to the next generation.

Proposition Five: We must offer Millennials an identity.

The excellent news for Millennials is that what Jesus did on the Cross is the solution to their identity moratorium.

Christ came to define Millennials and give them true purpose. Does our past define us? Do circumstances determine our identity? Do others' opinions appraise our value? Do Facebook, Instagram, or Twitter decide our fate?

On the cross, Christ defined us. He gave us an identity, and when we embrace that, we understand that our surroundings do not dictate our lives. God's Spirit inside us determines our destiny. Our circumstances do not control us. His covenant claims us as His own. The hell we may be going through cannot stop us. But the heaven we're going to has the final say. Our failures do not diminish us. His forgiveness finishes the story. We're not even judged by what we do for God. We're justified by what God has already done for us.

We find our identity in the Father, Son, and Holy Spirit. The Apostle Paul wrote, "My old self has been crucified with Christ. It is no longer I who live but Christ lives in me. So, I live in this earthly body, by trusting in the Son of God, who loved me and gave himself for me" (Galatians 2:20).

When Millennials know who Christ is, they will discover who they are. That's the reality of the gospel of Jesus Christ.

Proposition Six: We must create content that speaks to the heart, the head, and the hand.

Truth, logic, and common sense are under attack and on the precipice of death. Emotionalism has replaced them. Today it seems like Captain Kirk defeated Spock, and there is no rational Spock anymore, only Kirk.

We have to create content that speaks to the heart, the head, and the hand. Our content must inspire, inform, and impart.

As a church, we must focus on serving up messaging and resources that engage the next generation. We need to go all out with content that speaks truth to where they are. We must never sacrifice truth on the altar of expediency.

By the grace of God, our church family at New Seasons is multiethnic and multigenerational. We are 56% Millennial. We are 40% white, 40% Black, and 20% Latino, Asian, and Native American. We never water down the gospel. We preach the truth in everything, including gender, identity, and biblical, beautiful, holy sexuality. We don't water down the gospel, but we share truth with love, righteousness, and justice.

We need Christian leaders committed to biblical orthodoxy to produce content that will reconcile the vertical and horizontal planes of the Christian message and promote righteousness, justice, truth, and love for every community, every demographic, and every socioeconomic group.

This is entirely doable—and Millennials hunger for it.

We need to get the message out. We must elevate the truth of the gospel and the love and grace of Jesus Christ. We cannot permit one narrative to occupy space, especially in the media. Let's not be quiet or complacent. Let's build a firewall that is multigenerational and multiethnic.

Proposition Seven: We must stop being intimidated by younger generations

I am a math geek and a Trekkie raised in a small town. My parents are not preachers or ministers, but when I was growing up, they would obligate me to go to church. I doubted everything I heard there. I was the quintessential agnostic, the math guy who was analytical about everything and saw snake oil salesmen in every pulpit.

My dad was a UAW blue-collar worker, a down-to-earth, stoic man. I was a product of the 1980s. *Miami Vice* was my show, and Don Johnson was my role model. I thought I was incredibly cool because I had a pastel blue suit and white shoes that I wore without socks.

Whenever my Mack-truck-building dad dropped me off at school, he would stop and say, "Before you leave, I have one more thing." Then he'd stick out his arm, place his hand on my shoulder, and say these few words, "Heavenly Father, cover him with the blood of Jesus, protect him from all evil, fulfill your purpose in his life, in Jesus' name. Amen."

I was, or so I thought, this super cool, cerebral kid stuck in a car with my uber-traditional, union-member dad who recited words that he seemed too reserved even to say. And I didn't believe a word of it. That 7:48 a.m. drop-off routine was highly uncomfortable for me. I had one word for it: awkward.

After high school, I left home to study computer engineering at Penn State. One day in a quantum physics class, a brilliant Ivy League-educated professor introduced a mathematical equation showing the probability of randomness in the universe. He wasn't talking about God or Jesus. He just explained that believing we are here randomly requires immense faith—that the mathematical chances of randomness are so remote that they are almost to infinity.

That's the day I became a Christian. I didn't come to Jesus through a conference or a sermon, but through math, physics, and science.

Years later, I found myself in the White House with George W. Bush, being an advisor to the president because of the group I lead. They had called me. I had never called any of them. One day, I sat with Karl Rove and the President, then met with the Speaker of the House, then met with the Senate Majority Leader. I couldn't help thinking, *How in the world did I get here?*

I was sitting in the highest office in the land, fulfilling one of my life's purposes because of a dad who embraced the great news and dared to pray that it would take hold in a young man's heart. I had parents from another generation praying, even in front of me, that I'd realize that Jesus is the great news.

As I raised my three kids, every day I dropped them off at school, I'd say, "Before you get out of the car, I have one more thing. Heavenly Father, cover them with the blood of Jesus, protect them from all evil, fulfill your purpose in their lives, in Jesus' name. Amen."

My daughter blessed me with my first grandchild. When I got to the hospital to see little Liam, the first thing I did when they handed me my grandson was walk to the corner of the room and pray, "Heavenly Father, cover him with the blood of Jesus, protect him from all evil, and fulfill your purpose in his life." I wanted the first thing Liam heard from me to be the great news.

What's the great news? Jesus Christ.

Who are the Millennials in your life? Pledge to pray for them by name. Could you even summon the boldness to offer to pray for them in person? To bear their burden and lift to God those worries, fears, mental health struggles, feelings of purposelessness, or whatever might plague them?

What do we have to lose? Our pride?

And what do we have to gain? God's Kingdom come.

Christ's life inspires, His death redeems, His resurrection empowers, His grace suffices, His freedom completes, His joy strengthens, His spirit comforts, His goodness follows, His stripes heal, His name delivers, and His mercy endures forever.

Behold the Lamb of God.

If we will advance the Lamb's agenda, preach the message of freedom, exemplify both vertical and horizontal planes of the cross, recognize who we are and how much we have to give, offer Millennials the identity they'll only find in Christ, fill every channel with content that speaks to the heart, the head, and the hand, and stop being intimidated by the generation that we're supposed to reach, five to ten years from now, we could see a new Great Awakening in the Millennial generation.

The fact that we are occupying space on this planet in this critical time of human history is not by coincidence or luck. God has ordained us for this time. As you read this book, I pray that you will be convicted in your spirit that you are entirely able to be a conduit that brings repentance and the fullness of God's grace to this generation. I encourage you to proclaim the message

118

of righteousness, justice, truth, and love and impact the culture around you with humility and integrity.

Notes

1. George Barna, *Millennials in America* (Part I of this text), 13; 44; 14; 43.

DR. RALEIGH WASHINGTON

Asleep at the Wheel

Millennials are the largest generation of all time *and* the most godless. How did that happen? Who is responsible? How does this enormous population with no biblical understanding affect our culture now and in the future? And in our Millennial-dominant society of toxic divisions and false narratives, is there anything we can change?

I address these questions with hope and prayer that we who have been asleep at the wheel will wake up and address our nation's Millennial conundrum with poise, power, prayer, and proclamation of the voice of truth.

The most influential persons to sound that voice are pastors. And yet a supernatural shockwave is needed to ignite, encourage, motivate, and embolden our pastors to embrace this call. Pastors must join with other pastors to form that which is invincible—*the power of one*. Individual pastors have achieved great exploits for the Kingdom of God, but previous achievements will pale compared to what God will do for a lost generation if pastors unite in a voice of truth.

Is my description harsh or inflated? Not at all. Not when more than 50% of Millennials report mental or emotional issues, when 40% express gender

---

Dr. Raleigh Washington is president and CEO of Awakening the Voice of Truth. He is pastor emeritus and founder of Rock of Our Salvation (Evangelical Free Church), and also president emeritus of Promise Keepers.

or sexual confusion, when 39% identify in some way with the LBGTQ+ community; when four out of five do not consider life as sacred, when four out of 10 don't know God or believe in Him, and don't care to.[1]

Black Lives Matter

Millennials were born into a plethora of false narratives. One is Black Lives Matter (BLM), a toxic organization that capitalizes on its name and mantra, but whose agenda, in its leaders' own words, is anti-family, and pro-same-sex marriage. It is widely reported that BLM leaders are self-proclaimed trained Marxists who practice witchcraft.[2]

The vast majority of BLM protesters across the nation in 2020 and 2021 were Millennials solely concerned that Black lives truly matter—unaware that the group's real narrative is divisive and false.

Critical Race Theory

Critical Race Theory (CRT)[3] was developed in the late 1960s by a number of African American attorneys who wanted to teach that the United States was formed on white racism. CRT's recent revival builds on the premise that the residual effects of our national history negatively affect all African Americans, hence making them victims. This false narrative is driven largely by African Americans concluding in general that all whites are inherently racist.

In the 1940s, '50s, and '60s, a system of laws in the South known as Jim Crow mandated segregation between Blacks and whites, denying Blacks equal access in transportation, dining, public water fountains, bathrooms, and more. Blacks could not question the enforcement of the laws. Now the practice of CRT is Jim Crow in reverse.

Systemic Racism

I personally do not believe racism is systemic in the United States today. For it to be systemic, there must be laws that support or legalize discriminatory behavior as in the Jim Crow era. Today virtually no laws support discriminatory behavior. Instead, widespread voices across social media, certain press, radio, and television make accusations of racism, while other press outlets reveal the flaws and false premise of these accusations, leaving the impression that racism does not exist.

Racism does exist, but not in the system. It exists in the hearts of individual men and women willing to exploit a system to advance racist behavior. By this definition, which I believe is biblical, as an African American I can be as racist as any white person because the genesis of race hatred is found in the human heart. Today the accusations of racism are so widespread that they have lost meaning and validity. When an African American woman in Virginia wins the election for lieutenant governor and is called racist,[4] the accusation loses credibility. The discussion on racism needs balance. The Bible urges Christians to be sober in all things. The word "sober" means to be balanced, to give equal interpretation or evaluation on the differing sides of an issue. Balance gives credibility to a conclusion.

Transgenderism

A man will never be a woman and vice versa. Yet our nation, our government, and members of the Supreme Court believe multiple and transitory genders are reality. This ludicrous false narrative is taking our nation by storm. One journalist has reported that up to 10% of girls in public middle schools and high schools are claiming sudden onset of gender dysphoria.[5] Increasing numbers of those girls, though only in their teens, are getting irreversible sex-change operations. There seems to be a numbness to the catastrophic implications and dangers of the environment we are allowing for our girls.

The transgender false narrative is promoted by psychologists, psychiatrists, doctors, and leaders at the highest levels. This false narrative puts teenage girls in an endangered category.

Abortion

When abortion is portrayed as a woman's health issue, it simply cloaks the murder of the unborn. Our political climate is incredibly toxic. Democrats and Republicans do not just hate each other, they each seek to cancel the other, especially when it comes to the issue of abortion. The African-American race is currently in a state of genocide—and the direct cause is abortion. African-American women are 7% of the population yet represent more than 35% of all abortions. According to Walter B. Hoye II, preacher, activist, and author of *Leadership from the Inside Out*, a majority of African-American pastors are silent on abortion to avoid public controversy. Or their silence often is a response to private factors that complicate and implicate their own lives.[6]

This is the toxic cultural decline into which Millennials were born. These and other powerful false narratives have molded them into a generation confused mentally, emotionally, sexually, and spiritually.

The Solution We Need

As the generations that preceded Millennials, we must recognize that we bear responsibility for creating the environment they were born into and that now exists. To create a more positive atmosphere, we must tackle the task of destroying these false narratives. We must release the only weapon able to destroy what is false and work to create what must replace the toxic divisions. We must recognize the spiritual issues in our cultural decay and awaken the voice of truth.

I don't want to spiritualize the future to make it appear out of reach. Rather, I want to identify the spiritual battle that exists so that we will recognize how to address the false narratives.

What we face is the classic battle between Satan and Jesus. John 8 describes Satan as a murderer, a liar, and the father of lies. Satan's single aim is to deceive and destroy; from a splinter of truth, he can erect an entire false narrative. He did it in the garden with Adam and Eve, and the result was the fall of humankind. He attempted it with Jesus in the wilderness and failed miserably. Instead, Jesus defeated the tempter's deceptions, not with His authority or His power but rather with truth—His very essence. Today we desperately need pastors who are commissioned by God to sound the voice of truth. Pastors are called and equipped with truth, which is the Word of God, to address and destroy the false narratives that threaten to destroy us.

One can hardly deny that the Millennial Generation, the largest and the most godless generation, desperately needs the voice of truth. And yet the condition of pastors is perilous. As Dr. Barna's research reveals that 60% of senior pastors in the United States do *not* have a biblical worldview.[7]

This statistic reflects a grave and growing problem among the very leaders we depend on to give the church a biblical worldview. The problems that plague Millennials demand strong and clear teaching in the home, the church, and Christian colleges and universities. And yet in all three of these critical arenas, we fall short in espousing a biblical worldview, creating the single most devastating deficit of this generation. Simply put, the home, the church, and the Christian university need to be awakened to see their failing in this critical area.

There is a desperate need for pastors to address the false narratives behind the toxic divisions throughout our nation. During the two-year period of the worldwide COVID-19 pandemic and following the death of George Floyd, there arose a negative and devastating atmosphere. Across the country, protests spiraled into riots. Accusations of racism were rampant. The growth of cancel culture accelerated.

Civil discourse or civil disagreement over virtually any topic became forbidden. The toxic atmosphere allowed no difference of opinion or interpretation, or simply another position. There could be no discussion or mediation to a logical, objective, or sensible conclusion. The tone of the atmosphere was, "If I disagree with you, I am right and you are wrong; therefore, you must be canceled, eliminated, dismissed."

In the cancel atmosphere there is no room for forgiveness. If a person makes a mistake and apologizes for that mistake, that person is not forgiven and restored. The apology is despised or ignored, and the person is dismissed. In the cancel culture, people lose their jobs. Athletes are fined and suspended. Executives are fired. All because they made a statement that someone who does not even know the speaker interprets to be unacceptable, or racist, or insensitive. And the interpretations normally are driven by the court of public opinion. From there, angry divisions form in corporations, schools, churches, and even in families.

In the atmosphere of the cancel culture, almost anyone can say he or she is offended by someone else's words or actions. If the court of opinion sides with the person claiming to be offended, the offender is simply canceled. That has given momentum to the advancement of CRT, which is being taught in the government, military, and secular colleges and universities, and, sadly, even in some churches. The fundamental problem with the CRT dynamic is that there is no room for forgiveness and restoration.

That reality alone renders the cancel culture non-biblical. The Bible is based on truth, repentance, and forgiveness. In the current culture, there is no room to repent and be forgiven. Therefore, there is no truth according to the Word of God. This is the atmosphere in which Millennials became adults. This atmosphere, devoid of forgiveness, has been the source of toxicity dividing our culture. All of this is counter to the basic teachings of the Word of God. This platform in the current culture begs to be awakened by the voice of truth. Romans 3 tells us to let God be found true and every person be found a liar. Simply put, the moral code of the Bible is based on the truth in the Word of God. This truth has never been more needed than in this hour. The only salvation for Millennials, the largest generation ever, is for them to be confronted with the voice of truth. At the same time, the toxic nature of our culture today makes it difficult for pastors to preach the truth because it is in direct opposition to the false narratives swirling around us.

Pastors' Reluctance

Several roadblocks must be overcome for pastors to become the catalysts of awakening the voice of truth. At the top of the list is fear. There's an incredible amount of fear for pastors who preach the truth in opposition to what the secular community decides is fact. Transgender insanity has the support of the highest offices. Even the newest Supreme Court justice showed that fear when she avoided speaking the truth. In her Senate confirmation hearings when she was asked to define a woman, she declined to answer, saying she was not a biologist. She was staying within the latest parameters of these ever-changing cultural norms.[8]

Pastors are ordained to address matters that violate the Word of God, and yet they fear being accused of creating controversy in their congregations. The hour is such that pastors must step up and speak the truth regardless of consequences. A guiding principle is that truth without love is brutality. Love without truth, however, is hypocrisy. Pastors ordained by God to speak and preach the truth in love should speak both truth and love without compromise.

Pastors will always be criticized. That comes with the territory. But in this climate of cancel culture, criticism is more dangerous than usual because enough criticism can result in the pastor's removal. Fear of criticism that leads to avoidance of speaking the truth only serves to strengthen the false narratives, and the culture remains toxic.

The agenda of cancelation is to silence. I have a very good white friend who wrote a powerful and biblically sound critique of CRT. Two African Americans in his organization, offended by certain phrases he used, expressed their displeasure to my friend's superiors. His superiors then "encouraged" him to only listen for several months, without speaking. In short, my friend was silenced because he spoke truth and an African American disagreed.

Another example is an African American baseball player who said in 2019 that he'd like to be like Jackie Robinson and bring fun back to baseball. Not long ago, a white professional baseball player on another team, in the spirit of that statement about Jackie Robinson, called out to him, "Hey, Jackie!" Instead of bringing fun to the moment as he'd said he intended, the African-American player took offense. He said the white player was putting him down, and public opinion arose on the Black player's behalf. The commissioner of baseball rejected the apology, and the white player was put on suspension.

I don't know the heart of either baseball player, but based on the public report, I think the white player was misunderstood and dealt a cruel injustice. The commissioner of baseball refused to acknowledge a place for repentance and forgiveness.

It is true that Blacks have been slighted in the past, but this issue is deeper than merely correcting someone now. That fits into the category of cancel culture. But it is a non-biblical and immoral judgment because it makes no room for forgiveness.

Losing Church Members

Another cause of fear and reticence by pastors is the possibility of losing their church members when addressing a controversial issue or false narrative. The fear of declining membership has no place in determining what a pastor preaches. If a pastor preaches the truth in love, the members who reject those words and depart in anger must deal with their own attitudes for ignoring the truth.

The role of a pastor is always under great scrutiny, but in the current cultural environment the scrutiny has never been more intense. And yet the call of a pastor must always supersede concern for fear, or criticism, or cancelation, or disagreement, because a pastor is called by God Almighty to preach with a voice of truth without compromise.

We are living in perilous times. Our culture is in chaos and the largest generation ever is on a pathway to destruction. What must we do to reverse the direction of this spiraling crisis? The answer lies in understanding where this cultural nosedive began—in the classic battle between Satan and Jesus. Simply put, our culture today is experiencing the classic battle between truth and lies.

If pastors will recognize their challenge to address the lies (false narratives) with the truth (the Word of God), they will know the targets and speak the solution. It is impossible for a false narrative to triumph over the Word of God. Satan cannot and will not prevail over Jesus. Pastors are called and equipped to be the voice of truth.

The toxic divisions must be replaced by genuine, authentic relationships. We see husbands against wives, brothers against brothers, Blacks against whites, Jews against Gentiles. Jesus tells us clearly that the two greatest commandments are to love God with all our hearts, minds, and strength and, equal to it, to love our neighbors as ourselves. He explains to us that the law and the prophets, meaning the entire Bible, depend on these two commandments. In other words, if we can consistently love God and love our neighbors as ourselves, we will satisfy all the commandments in the entire Bible.

Jesus devoted a very important prayer to relationship. In John 17:20-21, He says, "I do not pray for these alone but for those also who believe in Me through their word, that they will all be one just as We, Father, are one—I in You and You in Me, and they in Us, that the world may believe that You sent Me." Jesus is seeing that the world (Jews and Gentiles) will believe that He is the sent Messiah, if indeed the Jews who believe in Him and the Gentiles who believe in Him come together in authentic, genuine relationship. This would be the greatest harvest of souls ever.

Jesus not only prayed for relationship, but He also went to the Cross and died for relationship. And we see there's a priority in this. It's found in Ephesians 2:14-15, which says He is our peace, our Shalom, the Prince of Peace. He broke down the barrier, the dividing wall of hostility between the two groups (Jews and Gentiles), so that in Himself—meaning His work on the cross—He might make the two into one *new humanity*, thus establishing peace.

Jesus is saying that He went to the cross to destroy the enmity in the divisions that bring only death. First to destroy the enmity between God and humanity—all of us—and second to destroy the enmity between the believing Jew and the believing Gentile, between the divisions in humanity. In so doing, the two would become, in relationship with one another, *one new humanity*.

The conclusion of this verse is critical because it says, "thus establishing peace." According to *Thayer's New Testament Thesaurus*, the definition of "peace" in this verse (*eirenes* in Greek)—is a state of national tranquility, particularly in a civil sense. It means the opposite of war and dissension; it means peace of mind, peace arising from reconciliation with God, and a divine sense of favor.[9]

In summary and in conclusion, false narratives that have created toxic divisions can be destroyed by awakening the voice of truth. Application of the Word of God can replace the divisions with genuine, authentic relationships, resulting in a state of national tranquility.

Notes

1. George Barna, *Millennials in America* (Part I of the text), 13-17.

2. Ryan Foley, "BLM leaders practice 'witchcraft' and summon dead spirits, Black activist claims," *Christian Post* online, Sept.1, 2020. Accessed at: https://www.christianpost.com/news/blm-leaders-practice-witchcraft-and-summon-dead-spirits-black-activist-warns.html.

3. For information about the history and development of Critical Race Theory, see: Kimberle Williams Crenshaw, "Twenty Years of Critical Race Theory: Looking back to Move Forward," *Connecticut Law Review* 43, no. 5 (July 2011): 1253-1354. Also: Jacey Fortin, "Critical Race Theory: A Brief History," *The New York Times*, Nov. 2, 2021. Accessed at: https://www.nytimes.com/article/what-is-critical-race-theory.html.

4. David Rutz and Brandon Gillespie, "Liberal MSNBC guest calls Winsome Sears a 'Black mouth' for 'White Supremacy practices,'" Fox News, Nov. 5, 2021. Accessed at: https://www.foxnews.com/media/liberal-dyson-msnbc-joy-reid-winsome-sears-black-mouth-white-supremacist.

5. Azeen Ghorayshi, "Report Reveals Sharp Rise in Transgender Young People in US," *The New York Times*, June 10, 2022. Accessed at: https://www.nytimes.com/2022/06/10/science/transgender-teenagers-national-survey.html.

6. Walter B. Hoye II, *Leadership from the Inside Out* (Maitland, FL: Xulon Press, 2005) 74; 33; 29; 49.

7. George Barna, "Release #05: Shocking Results Concerning the Worldview of Christian Pastors," *American Worldview Inventory 2022: A National Worldview*

Study of Parents and Pastors, Cultural Research Center at Arizona Christian University, May 10, 2022. Accessed at: https://www.arizonachristian.edu/wp-content/uploads/2022/05/AWVI2022_Release05_Digital.pdf

8. Myah Ward, "Blackburn to Jackson: Can you define 'the word woman'?" *Politico*, March 22, 2022. Accessed at: https://www.politico.com/news/2022/03/22/blackburn-jackson-define-the-word-woman-00019543

9. *Thayer's Greek-English Lexicon of the New Testament Thesaurus: Coded with Strong's Concordance Numbers* (Hendrickson Academic, Reissue, 1995).

LUCAS MILES

An Unchanging Something

In an effort to discover the meaning of reality, the pre-Socratic Greek philosopher Thales[1] proposed that water was the basic building block of the material world. He called it an "unchanging something." For Thales, water was an elemental thread that held the secret to the meaning and formation of the universe. While his theory didn't hold true, it did mark, according to Aristotle, the start of philosophical thought and arguably the beginning of the Western way of thinking.

Since the days of the Greek sages, human beings have sought meaning and purpose through philosophical ponderings. But unlike Thales' search, it appears that America's younger generations, Millennials and Gen Z, have traded the pursuit of an "unchanging something" for a search of a constantly changing "nothing." A belief in an infinitude of human genders, the creation of so-called "safe spaces," and Millennials' ill-advised acceptance of socialism over capitalism are all examples of the generation's attempt to find significance in a barrage of finite and lifeless human inventions.

Lucas Miles addresses some of the most challenging topics in theology, politics, and culture. Miles is the host of Epoch Times' hit show, Church and State with Lucas Miles, *and author of the best-selling book,* The Christian Left: How Liberal Thought Has Hijacked the Church.

Despite their complexities, these progressive machinations, rooted in notions of security and pleasure, can be defined as "nothings." None of these notions possess any eternal significance. This is one of the reasons why progressive ideas must also constantly change. Their evanescence and finitude require a constant evolution of thought to reinvent themselves until new ideas run their course and fizzle into oblivion, starting the process all over again. What remains is an empty and evolving theorem, a "constantly changing nothing" which no matter how hard one tries can never provide the security and pleasure that the Millennial generation seeks.

It is no wonder why. According to research from Dr. George Barna, 54% of young adults self-report "often feeling anxious, depressed, or unsafe."[2] When your entire reality is built upon a house of cards, stability will always be lacking. With that said, Millennials didn't lay these shaky foundations on their own—they inherited most of them. The generation was shaped by a perfectly blended sequence of historic events, charismatic leftist idealogues, and an agenda-driven popular culture determined to steer America's youth away from its long-held pillars of family, faith, and freedom.

Events of the last two decades, combined with alluring progressive figures and a rise in religious deconstructionists, have created the perfect storm of Millennials abandoning the once-trusted institutions of medicine, government, and religion. Events like 9/11, the Afghanistan War, the sexual abuse scandal that rocked the Catholic Church, the legalization of gay marriage, and COVID-19, with leadership from the likes of Barack Obama and Bernie Sanders and teachings of Richard Dawkins, Richard Rohr, and Rob Bell, have taken their toll. Whereas past generations turned to doctors, political leaders, and pastors for hope and insight, the Millennial Generation witnessed what they perceived to be the erosion of credibility for these former cultural pillars. Doctors became viewed as unreliable, politicians as power hungry, and pastors and priests as predators. Disenfranchised and hopeless, an entire generation was forced to venture out in search of new constants and trustworthy voices.

All of this of course was by design, as Critical Theorists fitted with a Marxist agenda determined to dismantle the Western way of life in hopes of birthing from the ashes a communist utopia, complete with universal healthcare, sexual liberation for all, and the death of Christianity. While Marxists had long been entrenched with this plan, the Millennial generation finally gave them the perfect substrate that they required to plant their seed.

And now that this seed is planted and most Millennials have entered the workforce, the generation known as "Gen We" is quickly remaking the nation in their own image. From redefining corporate America, our understanding of mental health, and even rethinking the role of the church, Millennials, with their emphasis on collective engagement, diversity, frugality, and distrust of hierarchical systems, are leaving an indelible mark on society. While many of these new cultural dynamics inspired by Millennials are positive, such as technological innovations that allow for remote work and increased family time and the introduction of anti-bullying campaigns in schools and the workplace,[3] their collective moral relativism and struggle to find a true north has allowed more insidious ideologies to gain a foothold within their ethos.

In an effort to understand this cultural crisis (largely shaped by Critical Theory) and prevent its cancerous spread to future generations, we will look at three specific "constantly changing nothings" in which Millennials have sought to find happiness and a sense of security: the environment, human sexuality, and the state.

Earthly Sanctuary

> You have stolen my dreams and my childhood with your empty words. And yet I'm one of the lucky ones. People are suffering. People are dying. Entire ecosystems are collapsing. We are in the beginning of a mass extinction, and all you can talk about is money and fairy tales of eternal economic growth. How dare you![4]

This is what Swedish climate-change warrior Greta Thunberg shouted at the world during the 2019 UN Climate Action Summit. The speech from Thunberg, who describes herself on Instagram as a "climate and environmental activist with Asperger's,"[5] drew the attention of global leaders and catapulted her to fame on the world stage. Thunberg, known for her dramatic words and sky-is-falling rhetoric, didn't just catch the attention of world leaders, but young people as well. In fact, according to one study, Gen Z (labeled the "Greta Generation") found that more 12- to 15-year-olds prioritized caring for the planet more highly than fashion or friends, marking a new trend in today's youth.[6]

Driving this increased concern for the environment in Millennials and Gen Z is likely their diminished view of faith and religion. Although previous generations placed more faith in heaven or an afterlife, today's younger, less-religious generations look for their security in an earthly sanctuary. One of Dr. Barna's reports on Millennials, "Indifference to God, Jesus and the Bible Drives Millennial's Faith," found that "Many young Americans neither believe that Jesus is the central figure in determining the nature of our eternal destination nor worry about the existence and nature of an afterlife." [7]

When society has lost hope for, as Augustine describes, "that kingdom which has no end," [8] it's only natural for individuals to begin to look for an alternative to that kingdom within the realm of mortal men. As this generation has turned from God, its gaze has turned to the Earth to solve the problem of human impermanence. With this in mind, we see that the Millennial obsession with health food, environmental activism, COVID protective measures, and reducing carbon emissions arises from the generation's disenchantment with heaven. Although Christian teaching promotes conservation and stewardship of one's physical body and the environment, the Millennial mindset has progressed past conservation into all-out global self-preservation as a way to postpone eternal extinction.

Contrasting the futile attempts of transforming this world into our eternal abode, the Apostle Paul warns:

> What I mean, brothers and sisters, is that the time is short. From now on those who have wives should live as if they do not; those who mourn, as if they did not; those who are happy, as if they were not; those who buy something, as if it were not theirs to keep; those who use the things of the world, as if not engrossed in them. For this world in its present form is passing away. (1 Corinthians 7:29-31) [9]

Of course, Scriptures like this shouldn't be manipulated to defend poor stewardship of the planet. As Christians, there is no reason to oppose improved waste-management solutions, the protection of endangered animals, or technological innovations that legitimately and economically reduce our reliance on fossil fuels. God created this Earth, and we were designed to "rule over the fish in the sea and the birds in the sky and over every living creature that moves on the ground" (Genesis 1:28). Part of rulership entails protection and conservation. America's younger generations need to see the church embrace these roles. But to do so, the church must never lose sight of the fact that "here we do not have an enduring city, but we are looking for the city that is to come" (Hebrews 13:4).

Additionally, climate activism like Thunberg's reveals a massive distrust of God and His faithfulness to oversee the foundations and framework of the Earth. The subtext is that God—if He even exists—isn't able to create a world capable of sustaining His children; therefore, we must take on the task. In an equally massive display of arrogance, power-hungry zealots have fooled a generation into thinking they possess the power to control the fate of a planet. In a similar exhibition, Job challenged God's integrity and power, and God leveled his pride by asking:

Who is this that obscures my plans with words without knowledge? Brace yourself like a man; I will question you, and you shall answer me. Where were you when I laid the earth's foundation? Tell me, if you understand. Who marked off its dimensions? Surely you know! Who stretched a measuring line across it? On what were its footings set, or who laid its cornerstone—while the morning stars sang together, and all the angels shouted for joy? (Job 38:1-7)

Until America's younger generations recognize that God's sovereign hand is sustaining His creation until the appointed time of His return, they will continue to look for safety and security through their own efforts. Ultimately, this is a fool's pursuit. And it is the first "constantly changing nothing" that the Church must address in this generation.

Sex and Gender

On June 26, 2015, the Obama Administration projected the colors of the gay pride rainbow flag upon the White House in support of a historic ruling that legalized same-sex marriage in all 50 states. Hardly an innocuous ruling, it opened the door for a litany of sexually variegated civil and cultural allowances. What began as a cry for equal rights snowballed into an assault against Judeo-Christian values and the heteronormative family. Erupting across the nation following this event were "drag queen story times," reports of men using women's restrooms, and a woke beauty company's 2016 debut of their first male "Covergirl," a minor named James Charles.[10]

Fast forward seven years, and America today looks more like the "Island of Misfit Toys" than it does the Land of Liberty. According to Tumblr.com, there are now 112 distinct genders. The list reads like a roll call of distant celestial constellations, with terms like astralgender, autigender, boyflux and cloudgender.[11] It's no wonder that Dr. Barna's research found that nearly one-third of the Millennial cohort (30%) describes itself as LGBTQ.[12]

That such a staggering percentage of Millennials (more than three times than in the general population) identify with divergent forms of gender and sexuality reveals how thoroughly critical pedagogy and a Hollywood culture bent on grooming children to be sexually active and diverse have corrupted this generation. In fact, such statistically anomalous percentages nearly eradicate the "born-this-way" argument of past generations. Even if genetic predisposition toward same-sex attraction were possible, to see this in one-third of the population is impossible through nature alone. This leaves only one explanation: The Millennial Generation has been programmed and persuaded to adopt sexual perversion as a way to find purpose, meaning, and happiness in life.

To demonstrate just how far the progressive agenda has advanced since the rainbow spotlight on the White House, one Millennial Tik Tokker recently declared: "Super straight is the 'All Lives Matter' of sexualities. It's not a real sexuality. It literally is just something that's made up to make fun of trans people."[13] In less than 10 years, traditional family values have been transformed from the societal norm to a fictional ploy designed to oppress the "real" sexualities, like transgenderism.

Attacks like this reveal a new form of critical thought, Critical Queer Theory. Like other Critical Theories, Critical Queer Theory divides humanity between oppressor and oppressed, by positing heterosexuals as sexual dictators heaping abuse upon the powerless sexually non-normatives. Offering a working definition of the term Critical Queer Theory, the course description for a class called "Introduction to Queer Theory" on the University of Massachusetts website reads:

Queer Theory destabilizes sexual and gender identities allowing and encouraging multiple, unfettered interpretations of cultural phenomena. It predicates that all sexual behaviors and gender expressions, all concepts linking such to prescribed, associated identities, and their categorization into "normal" or "deviant" sexualities or gender, are constructed socially and generate modes of social meaning. Queer theory follows and expands upon feminist theory by refusing the belief that sexuality and gender identity are essentialist categories determined by biology that can thus be empirically judged by fixed standards of morality and "truth."[14]

Notice that the course description concludes by reinforcing the idea that there are no "fixed standards of morality and 'truth.'" This distinction is important, as it demonstrates the religious framework that permeates progressive views of sexuality. Queer Theory isn't just an ideology, it's a religion. Bent on sexually evangelizing the Millennial Generation, the reality is that Queer Theory, the real cultural aggressor, would travel over land and sea to win a single convert, especially if it means convincing (a.k.a. grooming) a young person to shoot up with hormones or mutilate their body for the sake of the cause.

Millennials unaffected directly by the impact of Critical Queer Theory find themselves in the crosshairs of another form of over-sexualization through the nearly $100-billion-a-year pornography industry. It's not enough that social media outlets such as Instagram and Twitter offer nearly constant access to free pornography, now college campuses are adding to the increase of depravity by offering porn courses. Westminster College, for example, offers GNDR*3000, described in the syllabus this way:

Hard-core pornography is as American as apple pie and more popular than Sunday night football. Our approach to this billion-dollar industry is as both a cultural phenomenon that reflects and reinforces sexual inequalities (but holds the potential to challenge sexual and gender norms) and as an art form that requires serious contemplation. We will watch pornographic films together and discuss the sexualization of race, class, and gender and as an experimental, radical art form.[15]

Once again, buried within this sexual exploitation of students is the Marxist attempt to subdivide civilization by race, class, and gender. There have always been debaucherous back-alleyways of society. But when these alleyways wind their way through the nation's state-funded and public educational systems, this is cause for outrage. The absence of outrage from Millennials and Gen Xers against being subjected to this morally bankrupt institutional despotism shows just how long it's been in place. To reverse this kind of cultural Stockholm Syndrome within generations victimized by sexual groomers, America's church, conservative institutions, faith-filled and freedom-loving corporations, and God-fearing families must be prepared to model and demonstrate righteousness within society. But they also must offer well-produced and captivating alternative media content to educate, entertain, and enlighten a generation that has spent far too long subconsciously chained to Hollywood's agenda-driven programming.

Even more importantly, if the church is to win the culture war over the sexual distortion of America's youth, we must find new ways to cultivate identity and Christ-consciousness in individuals. But this will only be possible if we first successfully expose the misplaced lordship bestowed upon the state.

Millennials and the State

"Capitalism needs to evolve dramatically,"[16] writes Afdhel Aziz, co-founder and chief purpose officer of Conspiracy of Love, a global firm that consults Fortune 500 brands on issues related to corporate purpose.

Offering support for Aziz's statement is evidence that Millennials and Gen Z (as high as 52%) say they would prefer to live in a socialist or communist nation over a capitalist society.[17] It's unlikely that many of these individuals are students of Lenin or Mao. So, what is really behind this misguided societal shift away from meritocracy and towards greater entitlements? Simply put, America's younger generations are searching for purpose—and many are finding it in the form of social activism.

Filling this need for Millennials are radical groups, such as Black Lives Matter and Democratic Socialists of America. Marching alongside these nonprofits are woke corporations, which have embraced environmental and social governance efforts (which are a Western nod to China's social credit score). They've even aligned with Big Tech and the Biden Administration's newly formed Disinformation Governance Board (which is being compared to Hitler's Ministry of Propaganda and Public Enlightenment). Topping the priorities for these strategic alliances are facilitating entitlements and controlling the narrative, both of which require governmental tyranny to mandate and keep in check.

Never letting a good crisis go to waste, Marxist groups create chaos in the streets to pressure deep-pocketed organizations, prone to virtue signaling, to cough up millions of dollars to "solve" the particular injustice. Those who don't get on board face shakedowns, being heckled, and, if needed, protests until they either donate or cower in fear. Meanwhile, social media outlets ban any who ask questions and restrict content in order to facilitate the "right perspective" on the issue. Finally, the real powerbrokers, the political elite, present salvific policies supposed to correct injustice, but in reality, only give the governing autocrats more power to mandate the affairs of their constituents. When not marching alongside others in protest, Millennials have another crucial part to play in the ruse—posting on social media identifying images or colors to signify their allegiance to the cause. The few brave Millennials able to see through this social scam are typically bombarded with insults, pressured by their peers, and when bad enough, they're doxxed.[18]

This pattern plays out in scenario after scenario—the death of George Floyd, U.S. detention of child migrants, COVID-19 (including mask and vaccine mandates), the war in Ukraine, and many others. In hindsight, many of these instances were built around fake news, partial information, or the suppression of the truth. Millennials and Gen Z, indoctrinated by a strong revisionist history of the Constitution, the founding of America, and even the Bible, are easily persuaded by the Left's agenda. They gladly bow to the state with a zeal that would make even the Hitlerjugend jealous. And why wouldn't they? With the promise of free healthcare, college debt forgiveness, and utopian dreams of a futuristic society where everyone reads Hegel and drives an electric car, who wouldn't sell their soul?

Not even church-going Millennials are exempt from the onslaught of leftist propaganda. Equipped with convincing spiritual rhetoric such as "Love your neighbor" and "Jesus was a socialist," the Christian Left within the church joins in the chorus with religious agitprop, espousing a moral superiority over their non-woke brothers and sisters in Christ.

Peter Dreier, a self-described "cheerleader for social justice," postulates this very idea in an article for *HuffPost*, "Jesus Was A Socialist":

> It is worth remembering that Jesus was a socialist. Of course, he was born long before the rise of industrial capitalism in the 19th century, but his radical ideas have influenced many critics of capitalism, including many prominent socialists and even Pope Francis.[19]

Apparently lost on social activists like Dreier are Jesus' teachings on personal responsibility and personal stewardship, both of which are antithetical to socialist ideology. Consider the parable of the bags of gold, in which Jesus tells of a master who entrusted his wealth to three of his servants. To one he gave five bags of gold, another two bags, and the last one he gave only one bag. The first two servants doubled the master's investment, while the last servant gained nothing, to which the master replied in Matthew 25:

> You wicked, lazy servant! So, you knew that I harvest where I have not sown and gather where I have not scattered seed? Well then, you should have put my money on deposit with the bankers, so that when I returned, I would have received it back with interest. So, take the bag of gold from him and give it to the one who has ten bags. For whoever has will be given more, and they will have an abundance. Whoever does not have, even what they have will be taken from them. And throw that worthless servant outside, into the darkness, where there will be weeping and gnashing of teeth. (Matthew 25: 26-30)

Here Jesus demonstrates individual ownership and the value of individual stewardship of God's resources. He anachronistically refutes socialism, including the redistribution of wealth and the notion of social equity. Had a socialist written this passage, the master would have given all of the servants an equal investment from the start, while simultaneously distributing their reward equitably after the fact, regardless of their individual efforts. Parables such as this fill the New Testament. They provide conclusive evidence that the principles of socialism, which have led to the deaths of more than 100 million people in the last century, are void of any biblical credence and run contrary to Jesus' teachings.

Agnosto Theo

Millennials may be searching for happiness and security among the lifeless idols of earthly sanctuary, sexuality, and the state, but this doesn't mean their pursuit is inherently wrong. While these "constantly changing nothings" can never provide the outcomes they seek, the very fact that they are searching for more enlightened objectives than some previous generations should provide hope that not all is lost.

In Acts 17, Paul reminds the Athenians of the altar in the Areopagus to the *agnosto theo*, the "unknown god." The church today must find ways to draw Millennials' gaze away from lesser gods and back to the person of Christ, who is yet unknown to a major percentage of their generation. For some, He remains an unknown god amid a graveyard of false idols. For others, He is a forgotten deity, whose empty tomb is shrouded by the weeds of worldly indoctrination and the mossy overgrowth of spiritual deconstructionism. If we are serious about reaching Millennials, we should emulate Paul's ways as he addressed the people of Athens. Rather than demeaning the ignorance of the crowd, Paul praised the Athenians' religious zeal and dignified their altars, as he "looked carefully" at their "objects of worship."

Though statistically the spiritual and emotional health of the Millennial and Gen Z generations looks bleak, the church will not change this through broad-stroked criticism or harsh generational insults. To be taken seriously, the church needs to study topics important to Millennials—Critical Race Theory, socialism, environmental issues, and gender identity—so that we can effectively communicate with them on these topics. And it's important to remember that not all Millennials are alike. Many brilliant and creative Millennial minds are fearlessly defending their faith, rebuking their generation, and overcoming stereotypes.

It's also paramount that Millennial passions are not dismissed as false deities or a "constantly changing nothing." Some Millennial causes are positive, as long as they don't conflict with the biblical worldview. Parents, mentors, and pastors should look for ways to steer these passions (such as climate activism or social justice) back within a Christ-centric framework—one that takes into consideration the work of the Cross, the redemption of man, and the restoration of all things through the ushering in of the Kingdom of our God.

Jesus Christ: The Unchanging Something

While sin has existed within society since the fall of the human race, Marxism has found a way to unionize depravity in the form of critical theories that have decimated America's younger generations. Distorting the truth leaves Millennials and Gen Z mining for eternal qualities in decaying institutions and ideologies unable to support the security that they seek. None of this makes Millennials ignorant, gullible, or less intellectually savvy than previous generations. If we continue to treat them that way, by making them the butt of every joke and minimizing their role in society, we can only expect the culture gap to increase.

The challenge for the church today and in the coming years is to identify new ways to introduce Millennials to the true "unchanging something"—Jesus Christ, who is the same yesterday, today, and forever (Hebrews 13:8). Only then will we begin to see a transformative revival sweep through our nation capable of reframing the worldview of our nation's youth.

NOTES

1. Thales of Miletus (c. 620 B.C.E. - c.546 B.C.E.) was an ancient Greek philosopher, mathematician, and scientist.

2. George Barna, *Millennials in America* (Part 1 of this text), 31.

3. Ruchinka Rylshyan, "Millennials Have the Power to Banish Workplace Bullying," *Forbes* Online, Sept. 23, 2013. Accessed at: https://www.forbes.com/sites/ruchikatulshyan/2013/09/13/millennials-have-the-power-to-banish-workplace-bullying/?sh=5aed158f7cca

4. Greta Thunberg, Speech at the United Nations Climate Action Summit, Full Transcript, NPR Blog, Sept. 23, 2019. Accessed at: https://www.npr.org/2019/09/23/763452863/transcript-greta-thunbergs-speech-at-the-u-n-climate-action-summit.

5. Thunberg, "Profile," *Instagram*, 2022, https://www.instagram.com/gretathunberg/

6. Kiran Bose, "Gen Z Kids are the 'Greta Generation," *Energy Live*, July 16, 2021. Accessed at: https://www.energylivenews.com/2021/07/16/gen-z-kids-are-the-greta-generation/

7. Barna, *Millennial Report 03*: "Indifference to God, Jesus and the Bible Drives Millennials' Faith," Cultural Research Center at Arizona Christian University, Dec. 7, 2021. Accessed at: https://www.arizonachristian.edu/wp-content/uploads/2021/12/CRC_Millennial_Report03_Digital_01_20211207.pdf

8. Augustine of Hippo, *City of God*, Book XXII (426 AD).

9. All Scripture references in this chapter are New International Version (NIV) translation unless otherwise indicated.

10. Stephanie Chan, "Meet CoverGirl's First CoverBoy: Social Media Star James Charles," *The Hollywood Reporter*, Oct. 11, 2016. Accessed at: https://www.hollywoodreporter.com/news/general-news/katy-perry-covergirl-announce-james-937215/

11. Dude, "Dude Asks: How Many Genders Are There In 2022?" *Dude Asks Q&A*, no publication date. Accessed at: https://dudeasks.com/how-many-genders-are-there-in-2022/

12. Barna, *Millennials In America*, 32.

13. Lucas Miles, @mrlucasmiles, "The next variation of critical theory you need to understand," March 28, 2022. Accessed at: https://www.tiktok.com/@mrlucasmiles/video/7080288142280019246

14. J. Jeanine Ruhsam, "WGSS 392Q: Introduction to Queer Theory Spring 2017," Online Syllabus, no publication date. Accessed at: https://www.umass.edu/wgss/sites/default/files/assets/wgss/ruhsam_-_wgss_392q_-_spring_2017_0.pdf.

15. Hollie Lewis, "3 Porn Classes Offered at Utah College," WSAV Channel 3, Salt Lake City, UT, April 2022. Accessed at: https://www.wsav.com/now/3-porn-classes-offered-at-utah-college/amp/.

16. Afdhel Aziz, "The Power of Purpose: The Business Case for Purpose (All the Data You Were Looking For Pt. 2)," Forbes Online, March 7, 2020. Accessed at: https://www.forbes.com/sites/afdhelaziz/2020/03/07/the-power-of-pur-

pose-the-business-case-for-purpose-all-the-data-you-were-looking-for-pt-2/?sh=25df4b3cf7a5

17. Luka Ladan, "Why Do So Many Millennials Embrace Socialism?" *Catalyst* website, Feb. 22, 2019. Accessed at: https://catalyst.independent.org/2019/02/22/why-do-so-many-millennials-embrace-socialism/?gclid=C-j0KCQjwl7qSBhD-ARIsACvV1X3UGbBsfBItz34vCgJTqaRlFFzPtxX-I16oKnZqBCMifRoHCkvhkqRIaArw1EALw_wcB

18. "Doxing" refers to when an individual or entity displays another's personal information online in hopes others will harass them into compliance.

19. Peter Drier, "Jesus Was a Socialist," *HuffPost* blog, Dec. 25, 2016 (revised Dec. 26, 2017). Accessed at: https://www.huffpost.com/entry/jesus-was-a-socialist_b_13854296

JASON JIMENEZ

Bringing Hope to the Spiritual Disillusionment of Millennials

I looked deep into his eyes and could see the pain and discomfort vexing Jaden.

Jaden, an older Millennial in his mid-30s, no longer subscribes to what he calls "Evangelical Christianity."

He now refers to himself as an "Exvangelical," a social movement heavily populated with Millennials who became disillusioned with the church and have since walked away from their childhood faith.

Jaden's story is a typical one. He grew up in the church and served at Christian summer camps throughout high school. He even baptized a few of his friends at his family's lake house one summer.

Jason Jimenez is a pastor, Christian apologist, and the founder of Stand Strong Ministries. He is a widely recognized worldview expert who specializes in cultural, philosophical, theological, and religious issues, and, as a national speaker, addresses numerous topics including objections to Christianity, the problem of evil and suffering, and the reliability of the Bible. He regularly partners with Summit Ministries, a national worldview organization. Jason has authored/co-authored several books including The Raging War of Ideas, Stand Strong America, The Bible's Answers to 100 of Life's Biggest Questions, Challenging Conversations, *and* Parenting Gen Z: Guiding Your Child in a Hostile Culture. *He and his wife, Celia, have four children and reside in North Carolina.*

Jaden's family had high hopes for his future. His parents raised him with the affirmation that he would do great things for the gospel.

"I still get upset when I think about the hypocrisy I saw from my parents and church leaders growing up," Jaden said as he freely shared his hurt over leaving the church several years ago.

I wish I could say that stories like Jaden's are rare among Millennials. But sadly, they are not.

As I write this chapter, I'm stricken with heartache over a young woman my wife and I know who "de-converted" from her faith along with her husband.

For anonymity, let's call her "Molly."

Molly's parents are a sweet and godly couple. They have been serving in their local church for over 30 years.

It didn't take long for them to notice that their daughter had a special gift.

Molly was blessed with a beautiful voice.

As one would expect, Molly pursued her passion for singing and received nothing but love and constant support from her parents.

By the time Molly was a sophomore in high school, she was offered the chance to be the worship leader for the youth band.

It was clear to everyone that she loved God and used the gift God gave her to bless others.

That was until she met her future husband.

It didn't take long after they married for the young couple to began to express their doubts about their faith to both sides of their families.

Naturally, my friends kept this private out of fear of what that might do to complicate the situation even more.

Well, things never got better for Molly and her husband.

After giving birth to their first child, they finally came out to their parents that they no longer believed Jesus Christ as Savior and Lord, and didn't want to raise their baby girl around the lies and deception of religion.

Given the weight and severity of the spiritual crisis we are seeing unfolding among Millennials and Gen Z, I don't doubt that you have stories equal to Jaden's and Molly's deconversion stories.

So, what do we do with the "Jadens" and "Mollys" that are our family members, coworkers, and friends?

Are we to give up on their generation, seeing that the rise of the "religiously unaffiliated" continues to amass more followers? Or are we to acknowledge the crisis before us and be willing to do whatever God has called us to do to engage Millennials with the gospel of Jesus Christ?

I remember the first time I came across some data regarding the decline of Christianity among Millennials.

At the time, I was serving at a small non-denominational church, working as their youth pastor. What surprised me the most was the number of doubts and questions Millennials had about their faith, the Bible, and the struggle to reconcile the exclusivity of Jesus's claims.

I began to maximize my efforts to figure out just how rampant the doubts were among Millennials. As I prepared sermons and hosted venues for parents and students, I kept coming against a credibility problem. Most of my Millennial students didn't believe that the Bible was the supreme and infallible Word of God.

They were all adorable kids and hungry to serve their communities and tell others about the love of Jesus. But only a small group of my parents and their kids wanted to study the Bible.

I will never forget this particular Thursday night at church.

I had just wrapped up an apologetic class, and one of the couples approached me to ask a few questions.

They started by complimenting me on the class and how much they were learning. But then, the couple began to scold me for teaching too much of the Bible.

Yes. You heard that right.

The couple felt that we needed to focus less on equipping families to *defend the faith* and put more time and energy into *building up the teens' self-esteem*.

The amount of biblical illiteracy exhibited by parents eventually led me to study apologetics. So much so that my wife and I left our family and church community in Tucson, Arizona, to study under the legendary Dr. Norman Geisler in Charlotte, North Carolina.

After several more years of working with Millennials, Dr. Geisler and I published a Christian apologetic Q & A book in our attempt to provide biblical responses to leading questions young people asked in our ministry travels.

In one of the questions, Dr. Geisler and I took a deeper dive into the makeup of Millennials and their reasons for abandoning Christianity. Although we may not know the primary cause of Millennials being "less Christian" than the generations that have gone before them, Dr. Geisler and I found there to be seven reasons consistently conveyed to us by Millennials[1]:

1. **False Conversions:** Many Millennials (ages 18 to 29) who claim to be Christians never had a true conversion to begin with. The pat Sunday school prayers that churches and revivals have people recite don't guarantee salvation. Many young people never come to a point where they truly believe in Jesus Christ (Acts 16:31), repent from their sins, and give their lives to God (Acts 3:19; 8:22).

2. **Lack of Transferable Faith:** The simple fact is that a large majority of Christian parents have done a poor job living out their faith and raising their children in the Bible (Ephesians 6:4). Many Millennials have been raised to be legalistic rather than to live a biblical life. There's been a greater emphasis on rewarding good behavior than on being obedient to God's Word. As a result, many young people rebel and fail to see the discipline of God's grace in their lives.

3. **Rejecting the Bible as the Word of God:** Doubts about the Bible and common objections about Christianity often get the best of Millennials. You would think that after being raised in a Christian home and attending church for years, most Millennials would have a strong faith in the Bible. But the fact is that they don't. When asked about this, young people say they never really felt they could express their doubts and concerns regarding Christianity at home or in the church. This caused a level of intellectual skepticism to sprout up and choke any roots of faith that may have been left.

4. **Disconnect Between Faith and Culture:** Millennials fail to see the connection faith has to culture. Their lack of involvement in the church damages their ability to connect faith to day-to-day life. When Millennials grow up, they have no idea the role faith should play in their careers, personal interests, or future lives.

5. **Hypocrisy and Compromise:** Hypocrisy and compromise in the church play a significant role in many Millennials abandoning the faith. They see the church as more concerned about money and membership than about teaching the Bible.

6. **Biblical Illiteracy:** The majority of Millennials are biblically illiterate. Most of them have neglected reading and applying the Bible. So, of course, when a competing belief or religion comes their way, Millennials are unable to defend the Christian faith. One way Satan has been able to do this is through the false teaching of naturalism—an ideology that teaches there is no God, absolute truth, meaning, or afterlife.

7. **Misunderstanding of Jesus:** Millennials have never actually been taught about the life, work, death, and resurrection of Jesus Christ. The focus has been more on the celebrity pastor than on the Savior, Jesus Christ. More time and resources have been devoted to launching more satellite campuses than to training up the next generation in the Word of God. The result: Millennials never encounter Jesus.

Considering these seven factors that explain (in part) the decline of Christianity within the Millennial Generation, we understand the massive spiritual crisis afflicting them.

Spiritual Crisis #1: Devoid of God and Truth

Accepting truth outside of their personal experience and opinions is not something most Millennials are willing to embrace.

"Truth is what you believe it to be. You have your truth, and I have mine."

That's the answer given to me after striking up a conversation with a young businessman while we sat next to each other before boarding our plane.

The idea that truth is absolute, objective, and universal is held in contempt in the postmodern culture we live in today.

When a person feels the need to believe in something, that belief originates from the framework of ideas. As those ideas materialize, they give birth to a particular worldview that will determine how the person thinks, acts, and lives.

With the denial of objective truth, Millennials are quick to believe in sentiments that hold no substance and are mesmerized by social justice initiatives that conceal their real agenda.

Today's enticement to placate personal preference as the way to determine truth has found its way as the mastery interpreter of reality and Christianity. Ultimately, humanity is free to choose and act however they desire because no absolutes exist to govern their affairs.

Though most Millennials affirm God's existence, an overwhelming majority reject the notion that God is truth and is the ultimate standard of justice. Therefore, you are left with Jesus as a way to God. Not *the only* way.

As mentioned above, a big reason the "religiously unaffiliated" has drastically risen among the Millennial population is due to the contradictions, hypocrisy, and biblical illiteracy repeatedly witnessed among their parents.

Despite holding to Christian beliefs, the parents failed to behave according to their religious convictions, resulting in the lack of transferring a grounded faith to their kids.

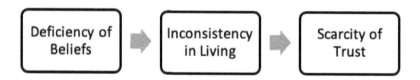

Deficiency of Beliefs → Inconsistency in Living → Scarcity of Trust

Currently, by all estimates, roughly 20% of Millennials self-identify as atheists. According to research from Dr. George Barna in November 2021, 41% of Millennials are what he terms "don'ts"—meaning they don't know if God exists, don't care if God exists, or don't believe that He exists.[2]

By his most recent count, 67% of Millennials claim to be Christians, but only 2% actually possess a biblical worldview.[3]

Casual Christians

When you take a closer look at Millennials who self-identify as Christian, the dominant group are, for lack of a better word, *casual Christians.*

Millennials have grown up with a kind of "Kardashian faith" that mirrors little of biblical Christianity. Half-sister to the Kardashians, Kendall Jenner, on her website, sums up perfectly the casual Christian's point of view:

I was definitely taught—even by my sisters—to believe in God. Also, to believe that He has a plan. Even though I'm more spiritual than religious, I pray every night and I 100% identify as Christian. It's most important to me, though, just to be good in your heart and do good in the world.[4]

Kendall's description of her faith is where we find most Millennials who self-identify as Christian. They are more spiritual in their beliefs with a sprinkle of Christianity on top.

Casual Christians have received a hefty dose of secularism and evolutionary theory that runs contrary to a biblical creation model. The indoctrination of naturalism has led Millennials to flock to mainline Christian denominations that are far more liberal in their views of the Bible, theology, and social issues. As Joe Dallas rightfully points out:

To these groups, binaries such as male and female are anathema. Traditional sexual mores are bigotry. Traditional evangelism is thinly disguised nationalism. The larger issues they believe we all should address include social justice, ending racism, slowing global warming, redistributing wealth, and ending all vestige of oppression. Enlightened people are expected to follow their lead in pursuing these goals above all others.[4]

Casual Christians have played a significant role in contributing to the decline of Christianity and its influence in the culture. They have refused to bring clarity to the gospel and avoid at every measure getting into exchanges that might be deemed offensive.

Spiritual Crisis #2: Bible Famine

When surveying Millennials, a minority believe that the Bible is a trusted and reliable source containing eternal truths. In 2014, the American Bible Society, InterVarsity Christian Fellowship, and the Barna Group commissioned an online survey of Millennials ranging in age from 18 through 30 in the United States.

The purpose of the survey was to provide a well-documented analysis of how Millennials view the Bible and their shift away from it as a sacred text. The research uncovered many alarming beliefs of Millennials. But one portion of the study stood out to me.

> More than six in 10 non-Christian Millennials have never read the Bible (62%), but what do they think about those who do read it? For most, it seems to evoke feelings of alienation and distance. When they see someone reading the Bible in public, non-Christian Millennials say they assume the Bible reader is politically conservative (22%), that they don't have anything in common with the person (21%), that the Bible reader is old fashioned (17%), or that they are trying to make a statement or be provocative (15%). Fewer than one in 10 non-Christian young adults indicate any kind of positive response, such as encouragement (7%) or joy (7%). Only 9% of non-Christians say they feel curious about what's in the Bible when they see someone reading it—a disappointing statistic for those who hope their Bible reading could spark spiritual conversation with non-Christians.[6]

And now, the recent data issued by the Cultural Research Center shows that only 29% of Millennials have a "very positive" opinion of the Bible, and a meager percentage look to the Bible as their primary source to guide them to make the right moral decisions.[7]

Spiritual Crisis #3: Directionless

I sat down with Trent, a 28-year-old math whiz and part-time YouTuber.

"It's been hard trying to figure out what I'm going to do for the rest of my life," said Trent with a stoic look.

I asked Trent if most of his friends feel the same way.

He nodded his head in agreement.

"What's causing you to be so stressed and worried about your future?" I asked.

Trent gave a few standard answers. Paying bills. Finding the right job. Stuff like that.

But I knew there was something more going on with Trent than he was letting on.

"Hey, Trent. Do you mind if I ask you something personal?"

"Sure," Trent answered, with a slight hesitation in his voice.

"When you get overwhelmed about work or paying bills, or even when you have to make an important decision in your life, how often do you talk to God about it?"

Trent looked me over before responding.

I think he was making sure he could trust me with what he was about to say.

"I don't know. Not much, I guess. I mean, I know I need to reconnect with God. And I'm lonely. I do need some divine intervention in my life because I'm directionless in my life right now."

When you factor in the Y2K scare in 2000, the terrorist attacks on September 11, 2001, the recession in 2008-2009, the trillions of dollars of government bailouts, the millions of jobs lost during the COVID pandemic, and record-high inflation, Millennials and Gen Z have had to reevaluate their careers and plans for the future.

Whether it's a single mom in her mid-30s trying to raise her kids right or a Starbucks-loving 20-something who finds himself in debt to his eyeballs in student loans, you will discover that 75% of Millennials are wandering through life dazed and confused about their purpose in life.[8]

But finding purpose and meaning in life goes much deeper than choosing the right career path.

Much of the confusion, frustration, and anxiety has led to a substantial increase in mental health issues and suicides.

The rise of mental health issues and suicides does, however, speak to the godlessness pervading this young generation.

In his monumental volume, *God, Revelation, and Authority*, legendary theologian Carl F. H. Henry poignantly characterizes the utter depravity that consumes a person's soul without God.

The modern loss of the God of the Bible has at the same time therefore involved a vanishing sense of human dependence on anything outside man himself; man sees himself as living on a planet devoid of any intrinsic plan and purpose, and supposedly born of a cosmic accident. He himself must originate and fashion whatever values there are. The current existential emphasis on man's freedom and will to become himself, particularly on freedom and responsibility as the very essence of human life, regards external authority as a repressive threat. Man's unlimited creative autonomy is exalted; this "authentic selfhood" consequently requires the rejection of all transcendently given absolute norms, for they are seen as life-draining encumbrances.[9]

The spiritual wantonness that besieges Millennials has reduced them to thinking their "authentic selfhood" is the best complement to living a happy and fulfilled life. And yet, the opposite of such pitiless aggrandizing emerges. Instead of being self-congratulatory for rejecting God and his moral absolutes, Millennials feel disoriented and are overcome by shame and regret.

All of this leaves Millennials hoping to find some form of satisfaction, whether in a relationship, spending hours upon hours on social media, or self-medicating to dull the emotional pain.

Spiritual Crisis #4: Faithless Parenting

The most staggering statistic I have read in recent years came from the Cultural Research Center at Arizona Christian University. In Dr. Barna's research, he found that only 2% of parents of children under 13 possess a biblical worldview.[10]

I have to say, when I read that stat, I was shocked, angry, and sad all at the same time.

Not only that, but the report went on to add that "parents who have biblical beliefs do not follow through with consistent, biblical behavior."[1]

Consider, for a moment, the profound implications this will have down the road.

Essentially, 98% of self-identified Christians are modeling and teaching their kids a nominal Christianity—at best!

In an intriguing piece, *Deseret News* put out new findings from the Survey Center on American Life that focuses on how busy family schedules leave no time for religion. The article states:

> In addition to creating a lot of stressed-out kids, modern parents' fixation on achievement is reshaping families' relationships with organized religion. Young adults today heard less about faith from their parents during childhood than previous generations and spent less time in church.[12]

Let's not be fooled when parents who profess to know Jesus also say they are too busy to attend church or can't find the time to read the Bible. They may *say* they believe, but their actions don't match their speech. That is a form of rejection—a rejection of Christianity.

If parents continue down this slippery slope, I fear there won't be many parents in the not-too-distant future who will be teaching their kids about the Christian faith.

Bridging the Spiritual Gap with Millennials

After examining the looming spiritual crisis of Millennials, it can seem next to impossible to do anything about it.

The reality of such facts about the loss of Christian influence in American society may cause you to feel dejected.

Which inevitably leads the church to retreat and give up on this troubled generation.

But don't let this trouble you. Let it inspire you.

For far too long, the older generations of Christians have taken their faith for granted.

From America's inception to its most formidable years, Christianity has been readily accessible and accepted as the primary position on moral and cultural issues, making the need to spread Christianity seem less of a priority.

As time passed, Christians became more complacent and apathetic to the gospel's advancement.

And now, in our current climate, Christians are not only the minority but are seen as outcasts and are feeling the effects of cancel culture at every turn.

Nevertheless, there is still hope.

We can't allow the scarcity of Christianity among Millennials to trigger a sense of defeat.

We must pray fervently and believe there is still hope for Millennials to come to Christ and live their lives with purpose and meaning.

So, let me give you some good news.

Despite the moral decline, Millennials still have an overwhelmingly high level of interest in spiritual matters.

In her grounded and thought-provoking book, *Is Believing in God Irrational?* Dr. Amy Orr-Ewing writes, "In a 'postmodern' society, spirituality is generally seen as a positive thing. People may not be signing up for organized religion in huge numbers, but many do believe in a valuable spiritual dimension to life." [13]

You will be pleasantly surprised how many young people would be open to discussing Christianity and learning answers to their objections and doubts.

Take that as a good sign as you seek to apply these three biblical steps to bridge the spiritual gap with Millennials.

Biblical Step #1:

Offer guidance and hope to Millennials who feel lost

Christians are given a mandate by Jesus to "make disciples" (Mark 16:25), and oh, how we have failed in fulfilling the Great Commission with the Millennial generation.

So, as you befriend Millennials, make sure to engage them in conversation around these important matters with clarity: (1) absolute truth, (2) objective morality, (3) gospel meaning, (4) true identity, and (5) dependability on God's Word.

Absolute Truth

The ancient Greek philosopher Aristotle affirmed that causes and effects (in reality) are known by and through first principles. First principles are self-evident truths. That is, they are metaphysical or fundamental truths that are assumed to be true.

With a bit of wit, Aristotle brilliantly demonstrates the undeniable reality of truth, "If you say that it is and it is, or you say that it isn't and it isn't, that's true. If you say that it isn't and it is, or you say that it is and it isn't, that's false."[14]

And yet, as mentioned earlier, Millennials have fallen for the lie that truth is a matter of opinion, not fact. Thus, they reject the nature of truth as absolute.

To point out the absurdity of such a belief, simply ask, *"Is it true that truth is a matter of opinion?"*

Notice the contradiction the Millennial will walk into if they say "Yes" or "No." For Millennials to deny the truth, they must affirm it.

The point is, start by politely challenging the relativistic thinking of Millennials and get them to recognize the truth about truth.

Hopefully, the door is open for you to discuss the truth claims of Christianity.

Objective Morality

Another area that Millennials desperately need to flesh out is their beliefs about morality.

When you look across the different generations, you will notice that Millennials and Gen Z rate statistically higher in believing that morals are relative.

So, as you engage Millennials about truth and morality, you must approach these conversations creatively by touching on their search for meaning and purpose.

It's noteworthy to mention that Millennials are often more charitable than their counterparts and anxiously looking to participate in a cause making a difference in the world.

You can show them passages like Romans 2:14-16, where the apostle Paul speaks of an objective and universal law that is binding on all human beings made in the image of God.

> For when Gentiles, who do not have the law, by nature do what the law requires, they are a law to themselves, even though they do not have the law. They show that the work of the law is written on their hearts, while their conscience also bears witness, and their conflicting thoughts accuse or even excuse them on that

day when, according to my gospel, God judges the secrets of men by Christ Jesus. (Romans 2:14-16)

Without compromise, Millennials need to see Christians stand up and defend objective truths about morality and clarify the value and reward for obeying God's commands, while, at the same time, talking openly about the consequences of not living morally before God.

Gospel Meaning

One thing is for sure. Millennials prefer a modern twist on Christianity that allows for a broader version of salvation that is syncretistic.[15]

However, that is not the gospel.

Jesus made it clear that He is the only way to God (John 14:6), and without Him, no one can be saved (2 Corinthians 5:21).

Don't be afraid to counter the false gospel presented by Millennials and make it clear what the Bible actually teaches.

It is Jesus who became our payment for the penalty of sin on the cross (1 Peter 2:24-25), rose again (Matthew 28), and offers salvation to anyone willing to receive Him as Savior by faith (John 1:12; Romans 10:9-10; Ephesians 2:8-9).

True Identity

It is an indisputable fact that Millennials are in an identity crisis.

They will take a plethora of personality tests, seek out identity in external things, and even venture into New Age spirituality to try and find their unique selves.

But what Millennials need is Jesus.

They need someone like you to teach them that they are:

- Image-bearers of God (Genesis 1:26-27; 9:6; 1 Corinthians 11:7).
- A new creation in Christ (2 Corinthians 5:17; Galatians 2:20).
- Uniquely gifted by God (1 Corinthians 12:4; Hebrews 2:4; Ephesians 4:7).

Amidst all the chaos over gender confusion, pronouns, and sexual orientation, we must empathize with Millennials and be proactive in having gospel conversations that point them back to their identity in Christ.

Dependability on God's Word

I will tell you the most effective and fruitful way to teach Millennials the Bible is to offer a small group Bible study in your home.

It doesn't need to be fancy.

Just be intentional and take risks recruiting a few young people and offer an authentic approach to engaging Scripture with them.

In 2 Timothy 3:16-17, Paul lists the benefits and blessings that come from being grounded in the Word of God. He writes, "All Scripture is breathed out by God and *profitable* for teaching, for reproof, for correction, and for *training* in righteousness, that the man of God may be *complete, equipped* for every good work." (Emphasis added)

As physical exercise is beneficial for your body, so too is the Word of God profitable for Christians as they are trained on forming proper behavioral habits so that they are qualified and able to live out their faith every day.

Biblical Step #2:

Model for Millennials a life of humility and the need for biblical community

The Millennial generation is tired of seeing hypocrisy running rampant among pastors who are supposed to be leading their churches as commanded in the Bible.

We need to stop relying on the machine of Evangelicalism to be the catalyst to reach Millennials with the gospel. Nor do Millennials need another big building or celebrity pastor to try and bring them to Christ.

What Millennials need is to see more Christians living out the words written by Paul, "Do nothing from selfish ambition or conceit, but in humility count others more significant than yourselves" (Philippians 2:3).

Millennials need someone willing to open their heart and home, and to display what it looks like to submit to God in all humility.

Millennials flock to people who are unpretentious, genuine, and level-headed. They need to see things as they are—no smoke and mirrors.

Invest in Biblical Community

Many Millennials struggling in their newfound faith didn't come from wholesome Christian backgrounds.

So, as we seek to teach Millennials the basics of the Christian faith, we need to help them build a community of trusted Christian friends who will offer much-needed support as they grow in their faith.[16]

At Summit Ministries, we firmly believe that strong faith comes by teaching God's truth and building lasting relationships.

Every year, students attend our summer programs looking for a safe place to be themselves and connect with Christians who aren't afraid to be vulnerable and willing to challenge their way of living and thinking.

Just taking the opportunity to open your life and inviting them into your community can do wonders for a Millennial who is on the fringe.

Biblical Step #3:

Teach Millennials how to go from a "fearful faith" to living a "fearless faith"

Meghan, who attends a very eclectic church in downtown Chicago, told me that her faith-sharing experiences have mostly been a waste of time.

Surprised by this, I asked if she wouldn't mind elaborating.

She thought for a moment and, with a bit of sass, replied, "Because, if I'm being honest, I think telling people about my faith casts a negative light. Either people think I'm proselytizing or judging them. I don't like that uncomfortable feeling, so now I choose not to speak up."

The truth is, Millennials are very reluctant to share their faith in public. Some think it's offensive to tell others about Jesus, while others, like Meghan, get uncomfortable and shut down.

A great number of things can be said about how to share one's faith. But in my years working with Millennials, I have come to rely on these three pieces of advice when helping Millennials share their faith.

The first piece of advice I share with Millennials is to give their fear over to God. Psalm 56:3-4 reads, "But when I am afraid, I will put my trust in you. I praise God for what he has promised. I trust in God, so why should I be afraid? What can mere mortals do to me?" (NLT)

It's far better to trust in God than to stand in fear of people. Left to themselves, all Millennials can produce is fearfulness. But left in the hands of God, they will exude fearlessness!

The second piece of advice I give Millennials is to learn not to get so easily offended when people disagree with them. Millennials tend to be insecure about their beliefs and would rather avoid conflict. But to grow in their faith and win over their peers, they've got to get over getting their feelings hurt. Jesus said, "Love your enemies and pray for those who persecute you" (Matthew 5:44).

The third piece of advice encourages Millennials to remain respectful and winsome when sharing their faith.

Millennials have seen too many of their parents and friends avoid talking about religion altogether or jump into conversations with an attitude that turned people off to Christianity. Therefore, teach Millennials how to conduct themselves in an open exchange of ideas that is Christ-like. Paul writes, "Let your speech always be gracious, seasoned with salt, so that you may know how you ought to answer each person" (Colossians 4:6).

As you and I reflect on the spiritual bleakness plaguing this generation, I pray that more men and women like you will bridge the spiritual gap that will bring more young people to experience the pleasure and eternal joy of Jesus Christ!

Notes

1. Norman L. Gusler and Jason Jimenez, *The Bible's Answers to 100 of Life's Biggest Questions* (Grand Rapids, MI: Baker Publishing Group, 2015), 271-272.

2. George Barna, *Millennials in America* (Part I of this text), 31.

3. Barna, "Release 01: The Worldview Dilemma of American Parents," *American Worldview Inventory 2022: A National Worldview Survey of Parents and Pastors*, 1. (Release Date: March 8, 2022). Accessed at: https://www.arizonachristian.edu/culturalresearchcenter/research/.

4. Lindsay Kimbell, "Kendall Jenner Opens Up About Her Faith: 'I Was Definitely Taught—Even By My Sisters—to Believe in God,'" May 9, 2016. https://people.com/tv/kendall-jenner-opens-up-about-her-faith/.

5. Joe Dallas, *Christians In a Cancel Culture: Speaking with Truth and Grace in a Hostile World*, (Eugene: OR: Harvest House Publishers, 2022), 148.

6. Barna Group, "Millennials and the Bible: 3 Surprising Insights," Oct. 21, 2014, https://www.barna.com/research/millennials-and-the-bible-3-surprising-insights/. Note: Dr. George Barna founded the Barna Group in 1984 (which he sold in 2009).

7. Barna, "Millennial Report 03: Indifference to God, Jesus and the Bible Drives Millennials' Faith," 7. (Release Date: Dec. 7, 2021). Accessed at: https://www.arizonachristian.edu/culturalresearchcenter/research/.

8. This is one of the key findings from Barna's *Millennials in America*, 16.

9. Carl F. H. Henry, God, Revelation, and Authority, Vol. 1. (Wheaton, IL: Crossway Books, 1999), 267.

10. Barna, "Release #02: The Strengths and Weaknesses of What Pre-Teen Parents Believe and Do," *American Worldview Inventory 2022: A National Worldview Survey of Parents and Pastors*, Cultural Research Center at Arizona Christian University, March 29, 2022, 1. Accessed at: https://www.arizonachristian.edu/wp-content/uploads/2022/03/AWVI2022_Release_02_Digital.pdf.

11. Ibid.

12. Kelsey Dallas, "Trying to Raise Successful Kids? Experts Say You Shouldn't Forget about Faith." *Deseret News,* April 8, 2022. Accessed at: https://www-deseret.com/faith/2022/4/7/23010246/trying-to-raise-successful-kids-heres-why-you-shouldnt-forget-about-faith-parenting-religion.

13. Amy Orr-Ewing, *Is Believing in God Irrational?* (Downers Grove, IL: Inter-Varsity Press, 2008), 30.

14. A paraphrase of Aristotle's "Correspondence Theory of Truth," Metaphysics, 1011b26 (350 BC).

15. According to Dr. Barna, 88% of Americans embrace a worldview known as Syncretism. "Rather than developing an internally consistent and philosophically coherent perspective on life, Americans embrace points of view or actions that feel comfortable or seem most convenient. Those beliefs and behaviors are often inconsistent, or even contradictory." See: "Report 01: America's Dominant Worldview—Syncretism," *American Worldview Inventory 2021: A National Survey of Biblical and Competing Worldviews*, Cultural Research Center at Arizona Christian University, April 13, 2021. Accessed at: https://www.arizonachristian.edu/culturalresearchcenter/research/. He discusses Syncretism among Millennials in *Millennials in America*, 48; 73.

16. Biblical community is made up of like-minded believers (Romans 12:5) who "build one another up" (1 Thessalonians 5:11) and "teach and admonish one another in all wisdom" (Colossians 3:16).

ISAAC CROCKETT

What to Do with a Generation that Rejects Absolute Truth

I graduated from high school in the year 2000 and consider myself an "O.M.,"
which stands for "Original Millennial" or "Older Millennial," although my
children tell me it just means "Old Man." For some it's hard to believe that
the generation known as "the Millennials" is not only the largest generation
in America, but it is also the generation of current parents. In many areas,
I fit the mold of the Millennial stereotype, while differing in significant
ways, too. One of the areas that I have been particularly cognizant of with
my generation is the spiritual crisis we're facing as a result of our worldview.

When I first started studying the *Millennials in America* report from Dr.
George Barna, I felt shocked to read that in my generation, "Only one third
of Millennials believe in God as the all-powerful, all-knowing, perfect and

Isaac Crockett is a pastor and co-host with Sam Rohrer on Stand in the Gap TV
and Stand in the Gap Today *radio program. Prior to coming to Stand in the
Gap media, he pastored for more than a decade and helped several church plants
and church revitalization projects. He recently completed a theology doctorate from
the Seminary of the College of the Open Bible and has done graduate work in the
areas of pastoral studies, social work, and family therapy at Bob Jones Seminary,
Drexel University College of Medicine, and Evangelical Seminary. He and his
wife home-educate their three children.*

just creator of the universe who still rules the universe today."[1] It was also sad to read that "three out of four Millennials believe that all religious faiths are of equal value."[2] I think this distancing from a biblical worldview is connected to what Dr. Barna discovered about our belief in absolute truth: "Most Millennials reject the existence of absolute moral truth and identify feelings, experiences, and advice from family and friends as their most trusted sources of moral guidance."[3]

It is important to know the facts about the problems in this generation if we are to seek biblical solutions. I am deeply thankful for the research in this area, but it is disappointing to see clearly that my generation has turned away from a biblical worldview.

I find it ironic that Alexander Solzhenitsyn, the Russian-born author who won the Nobel Prize in Literature and a staunch critic of Communism, warned our Western civilization of the consequences that follow when "men have forgotten God" in his famous Templeton Address.[4] The irony to me is that this address was made in 1983, about the same time researchers designate as the beginning of the Millennial Generation in America. Despite the clear warnings from Solzhenitsyn, my generation was, by and large, taught to forget God and pursue our own desires. This has taken us to a place of rejecting biblical absolute truth and following our own ideas instead of God's teachings.

In the late spring of 2020, while driving home from work that had taken me out of town, I saw something alarming on the side of the onramp to the highway. I carefully pulled my vehicle over to the shoulder and the car behind me slowed to a stop as well. I got out of my truck and turned to the people in the car who had obviously seen what I spotted. "Is that a human body back there?" I asked. As his wife picked up her phone, getting ready to dial 911, the man behind me stepped out of his car and walked with me to what appeared to be a man lying limply on top of a backpack and tool belt. The closer we came to the scene the more worried we were that this was a dead body. We saw no movement, despite hollering and shouting to see if assistance was needed. I knelt down next to the collapsed body of a young man and thanked God when I felt his pulse and slow breathing. As the other stranger and I huddled over him, the young man started to revive and asked us not to call the police. He assured us he only needed to get out of the sun and have something to drink. We helped him to my truck and found out he was trying to get to Corning, New York, the town I live in and where I was headed.

After making a stop at a nearby Taco Bell for the largest fountain drink they have and some food, we started the 30-mile trip home. As he guzzled his drink and devoured several chalupas and tacos, we began a friendly conversation. He told me how he had been working as a professional roofer until about a week earlier, when he argued with his boss and was fired. He was trying to walk home but was several states away and with the COVID-19 scare, he found it hard to catch many rides. I told him I thanked God he was alive and asked if I could pray for him. He was glad for me to pray for him, and it began a discussion about faith. He explained that he had grown up in a Christian home but after a family member was abused by someone in leadership in his church, he began doubting God's omnipotence and goodness. He told me he was still interested in spiritual things and that he was fascinated by many of the Eastern religions. He went on to describe what he saw as the commonalities with those New Age beliefs and some of the Christian beliefs he was taught as a child. The young man riding in my truck considered all faiths and religions to be equal because he thought they had a common goal of helping people find peace. He believed in some kind of higher spiritual power, but not in a personal or omnipotent creator God as the Bible teaches. Even though my belief was different than his, this young traveler felt we could both hold to our own beliefs as equally true.

As I reflect on that and other conversations I've had with folks my age and younger, I can see what the research points to. It seems strange to me that someone would believe in more than one truth. But if we set aside absolute truth, then we get to choose what is true to us personally no matter how different that truth is from that of the person next to us. This worldview has "forgotten God" as Solzhenitsyn warned in 1983, leading to confusion and despair. The spiritual crisis experienced in my generation seems to directly correlate to their worldview—one that has forgotten God and rejected absolute truth. Jesus instructs that He is the only way to God. In His teaching, He describes Himself as not only the way to God, but also the truth. It is significant that so many Millennials do not believe in absolute truth simply because of the claim that absolute truth is ultimately found only in the God of the Bible.

The situation that we are facing in America, particularly with our younger generations, did not happen in a vacuum. And it did not happen overnight. We have been on a dangerous trajectory much like what Solzhenitsyn observed, a slipping of generations from the biblical worldview to a rejection of the Bible and its truth. My generation was taught in public schools that the universe is here as a result of so-called natural causes and that we are here by what could be considered a cosmic accident rather than being created in the image of almighty God for His glory.

We also witnessed leaders both in politics and in the church go through very public moral failures during our childhood. As we watched famous politicians and pastors get caught in the webs of deceit and adultery, my generation lost trust in the institutions of government and church. We learned through experience that so-called experts can be very wrong. Many experts warned about major computer problems that would bring the world as we know it to a halt in what was called Y2K, yet nothing seemed to happen as we rang in the new millennium. We also watched experts in science fall woefully short on scary prophecies of global warming that have not matched their dire predictions from the 1990s and early 2000s. It is no surprise that my generation seems skeptical of many, if not most, authority figures.

Millennials also have been affected by modern personal computer technologies that developed rapidly during our childhood along with Internet technology With those technological advances in our early lives, we grew up in a world with access to more technology and information than generations before us. With this information came a sense of burden for all that is happening in the world. We have watched wars and natural disasters from all over the world unfold right before our eyes on the screens of our computers and smartphones. We were deeply affected by the September 11th attack on the World Trade Towers in 2001. With that attack we developed a fear that the unknown may strike when and where we least expect it. To understand all of these complicated situations, my generation needs to be grounded in an understanding of God's will for our lives and know His word more than ever. Yet we have rejected Him and His ways.

Authenticity and Consistency

How do we help Millennials and others who do not have a biblical worldview navigate this difficult time in history? Every culture and generation have tended to respond well to authenticity and consistency. In the New Testament church, Christians were instructed to be authentic and consistent, and that advice rings true for us in American churches today. One obvious way to influence Millennials is to get to know them and develop relationships in which they can trust us and relate to us. Within the context of the relationship, Millennials (or folks from any generation for that matter) can see what we believe and why we believe it.

Effectively reaching Millennials with biblical truth is not necessarily easy, but it can be done if we will follow biblical instruction and truth. In 1 Peter 3:8-22, we find some helpful guidance for sharing our faith in Jesus with people who have a different worldview. 1 Peter 3:15 explains what we sometimes refer to as apologetics: "But in your hearts revere Christ as Lord. Always be prepared to give an answer to everyone who asks you to give the reason for the hope that you have. But do this with gentleness and respect."

Here Peter explains that before we evangelize outwardly, we need to make sure of things inwardly. We must have an understanding of what our hope is and what makes our worldview different from others. He also assumes when we are among nonbelievers, the gospel hope that guides us and brings truth to our lives will stand out, causing them to ask why we have hope when they are hopeless. Finally, Peter instructs believers to handle this in a humble and respectful manner that reflects the gentleness of Christ. Throughout this chapter, Peter reminds us of what happened to Jesus and other believers. Our message can be rejected because following Jesus Christ exclusively is offensive to some. But we should never be offensive or abrasive. Instead, we should be winsome and peaceful. We should be prepared with apologetics but know that we cannot force our faith on someone else. The apostle Peter prepares us to be ready to have our message misunderstood and maligned by those who do not understand.

As followers of Christ, we are not commanded to force others to follow us, but to witness or testify of what we have learned from Christ. We can prepare for sharing the Gospel of Christ by knowing His Word. We can ask God to open doors of opportunity to form meaningful relationships with Millennials and others who may not have a biblical worldview. We can trust the Holy Spirit to give us wisdom on what to do and say to best represent Jesus and then trust that God will use us for His glory.

Knowing someone and having a trustworthy relationship with them are two separate things. We should pray and look for opportunities to befriend folks who believe differently than us. In the course of that relationship, we can ask God to help us be an object lesson of the biblical worldview. We also cannot share our worldview if we do not know what we believe, and we need to be able to communicate those beliefs to others. These teachings sound simple but require daily consistency and a humble trust in the Holy Spirit to guide and teach throughout the process. Reaching Millennials (or any other group) for Christ is impossible to do on our own. It does not help our case to try to blend in with worldly philosophies or methods. It does not work to hide the light of God from the darkness of this world. We must make ourselves vulnerable and open to God's will by trusting God to move in and through us. It is popular to focus on what sounds positive to those around us and hide the truth of God's Word. But we are called to live and give the full account of God's good news to those around us.

A number of years ago, my wife and I moved to northeastern Pennsylvania to assist a church planting team. While an assistant pastor, I also worked in the community doing social work. One job was at a residential home for troubled youth. I remember early on having troubles with one of the older boys, who was a high school senior and often the ringleader of getting into trouble. It bothered him that I was a pastor and he made it clear that he did not like me or my faith. I asked God to help me to be kind to him and develop a relationship where he might come to see Christ. It didn't seem he would ever want to be friends, but I did notice that he liked to take things that did not belong to him, oftentimes even when they held seemingly no value to him. I began bringing a study Bible with me in my personal bag. Sure enough, when I was working with one of the other boys, my Bible went missing. I had my suspicions of who may have taken my Bible and I prayed that the young person who took it might actually read it. In hopes of having more things stolen, I brought other booklets and tracts that I hoped would disappear—and they did. Soon I saw this same young man who had mocked me and given me trouble now studying my stolen Bible, sometimes for hours on end.

I did not know how to reach this young man, but I prayed that the Holy Spirit would work. As I sensed something miraculous happening, I prayed even more for the Holy Spirit to guide me. A few weeks later, the teen who had given me so much grief came to me looking much different and apologized. He admitted to stealing my Bible and some other books and wanted to return them. I checked with my boss and was allowed to give them to this young man. He told me that one of the other boys at the residence claimed to be a Christian and went to a church youth group and that he had been attending with his friend. One day this young man who had been such a troublemaker came to me with a big smile. He told me he had accepted Christ and was a changed person. I could see the Holy Spirit changing this new Christian. It was exciting to see him start sharing his faith with the others at the residence. I did not know what I was doing, but God did. He worked in the heart of the young man I was praying for.

Standing Out for God's Truth

There are times I feel like trying to fit in, but God calls us to stand for His truth. We will not reach this world with biblical truth if we camouflage it. Sometimes this means admitting when we have messed up. As a father, a pastor, a teacher, a friend, and in many other areas, I have messed up and seen God use the humiliation of admitting my failure to strengthen a relationship. When we admit that we are not perfect and that we are in need of help, it allows us to be authentic and develop realistic expectations and friendships with others. If you are looking for ways to reach the Millennial Generation that seems to have forgotten God, don't try to impress them with what you know or by trying to fit in. Instead, ask God for opportunities to point them to Him.

The Millennial generation is experiencing a deep spiritual crisis, but they are not the first generation to forget God. It is clear from Dr. Barna's research that my generation is confused and struggling because they have rejected God and His absolute truth. Let us pray that God will work to bring this generation and our entire nation back to Him and ask the Holy Spirit to guide us in reaching this generation with biblical truth. We cannot be afraid of what other people will say but should be concerned with what God has clearly told us to do. God has instructed us to go forth as His witnesses to all generations—and this especially includes the Millennials.

Notes

1. George Barna, *Millennials in America* (Part 1 of this text), 96.

2. Barna, *Millennials in America*, 43.

3. Barna, "Millennials in Spiritual Crisis and the Loss of the Biblical World-view," Millennial Panel 4, *Voice of Reason*, Foundations of Freedom, Jan. 31, 2022. Accessed at: https://www.arizonachristian.edu/culturalresearchcenter/resources/

4. Alexander Solzhenitsyn, "Acceptance Address by Mr. Aleksandr Solzhenitsyn," *Templeton Prize*, May 10, 1983. Accessed at: https://www.templeton-prize.org/laureate-sub/solzhenitsyn-acceptance-speech/.

KEN SANDE

Feed Millennials' Hunger for Relationships

Dr. George Barna's Millennial research reveals a number of troubling trends regarding this generation of Americans.

According to this study, only one third of Millennials believe in God as the all-powerful, all-knowing, perfect, and just creator and ruler of the universe. Most Millennials reject the existence of absolute moral truth. A majority of them are anxious, depressed, or fearful. And 39% of 18– to 24-year-olds identify as LGBTQ.[1]

But this study also reveals significant opportunities for meaningful ministry.

Although Millennials' most-desired change in life is for greater financial ease and comfort, that desire is followed closely by a longing for better, deeper friendships, fewer tensions with others, greater understanding and respect, a wider circle of reliable friends, and a better relationship with a spouse or significant other.

Ken Sande is the founder of Peacemaker Ministries and Relational Wisdom 360 (RW360). He is also the author of The Peacemaker: A Biblical Guide for Re-solving Personal Conflict, *which has sold over 500,000 copies in 20 languages. For more information on the relational and peacemaking skills summarized in this chapter, please visit www.rw360.org.*

In other words, right behind Millennials' desire for financial ease is a longing for deep, nurturing, and enduring relationships.

This longing is an echo from Eden, where God programmed into every human being not only a desire but also a fundamental need for relationship: "It is not good that man should be alone" (Genesis 2:18).

And just as it was God himself who programmed this desire and need into the human heart, it is God who has established the church as His primary channel for fulfilling this need (Ephesians 3:10-11).

The church is like a mobile food kitchen in a town where many of the people are hungry. Some only mildly so, but others are literally starving for the food that only Jesus Christ and His church can provide: a way to be forgiven and reconciled to God, and to experience loving relationships with those around us.

This relational hunger creates a wide-open door for Christians to engage, love, serve, and evangelize Millennials.

Begin with Repentance

Unfortunately, churches often are not seen as a place to go for loving, accepting, and nurturing relationships. As Dr. Barna and a team of researchers observed in a 2007 study, 85% of people who rejected Christianity did so because they viewed Christians as relationally hypocritical. We proclaim love and acceptance, but the world often sees us treating others in harsh, uncaring, and judgmental ways.[2]

Thus, the starting point for many Christians and churches is to confess to God that we have failed to live up to the relational standard Jesus set for us in John 13:34-35: "'A new commandment I give to you, that you love one another: just as I have loved you, you also are to love one another. By this all people will know that you are my disciples, if you have love for one another.'"

We then need to ask for His grace to enable us to truly repent of our relational failures, to put off our sinful ways of relating to others, to have our minds renewed, and to put on a new self that consistently manifests the likeness and relational characteristics of God (see Ephesians 4:22-24).

The Power of Personal Example

As God changes and empowers us to love others with the same kind of gentleness, kindness, patience, and forgiveness that He has shown to us, our example can have a powerful impact on others, including the Millennials we encounter in our day-to-day lives.

This is exactly how God got ahold of my heart and life. Although I was raised by a godly mother, had a sound Christian education, and lived a generally moral life, by the time I got to college, I was living my life according to my own ideas and goals with little concern for what God had put me on Earth to do.

Then God brought three deeply committed Christian men into my life during an engineering internship, graduate school, and my first job after graduation. None of these men lectured or preached to me; they simply lived out the relational characteristics of Christ in quiet and consistent ways in their daily lives. I was especially moved by the ways that they interacted with their wives and children. What I observed made me long for the same kind of affirming and affectionate marriage they so clearly enjoyed.

Being an engineer, I tried to analyze what I was seeing, to find the common denominators that were leading to such fulfilling relationships, both with coworkers in the office and with their families at home. It finally dawned on me that the single strongest common denominator was the fact that all three of these men and their wives were deeply committed Christians.

This realization moved me to return to church when I began law school. God graciously led me to a church where the gospel was clearly preached and the love of Christ was displayed regularly and consistently, not only in how the people loved, served, and encouraged one another when things were going well, but also in how they resolved their conflicts and preserved their relationships in a spirit of humility, gentleness, and forgiveness.

Realizing that these loving and healthy relationships were the fruit of the gospel, I soon put my trust in Jesus as my Savior and Lord and asked Him to begin working in me so that I could experience the same kind of relationships.

In short, one of the most important ways that Christians can serve Millennials today is to live out the relational fruit of the gospel—"love, joy, peace, patience, kindness, goodness, faithfulness, gentleness, and self-control"—in such a way that others will hunger for the same kind of relationships and be drawn to the source of this fruit, the Lord Jesus Christ.

Practical Relational Skills

The Bible is filled with instruction on how we can develop practical skills that improve our relationships and reveal the wisdom and power of Christ working in and through us. Learning and practicing these things day-in and day-out in the presence of Millennials God places in our lives is one of the best ways to open their eyes to the redeeming and transforming power of Christ and show them how they can satisfy their hunger for healthy relationships.

Here are just a few of the relational principles that I have found to be most useful in day-to-day life.

1. Pray for Special Grace

None of us can change our relational habits and develop Christ-like relational skills through our own efforts. The only way to experience significant and lasting change is by asking God every day to carry out a major ongoing transformation of our hearts and habits. For example:

> Lord, You know all too well how much my sinful tendencies undermine my relationships and weaken my witness for you. Please forgive me for my frequent failures to model the love of Christ and send Your Spirit into my heart today to empower me to live out Jesus' command to love others as You have loved me so that everyone who watches my life will know that I am Your disciple and hunger for You to work in their lives the way You are working in my life.

2. Bring the Gospel into Every Conflict

When Christians struggle with relationships, our tendency is to resort to "the law." We love to use God's Word to show where we're right and others are wrong. This approach only drives us further apart.

You can show people a better way. Instead of bringing the law to others, bring them the gospel. Share how the gospel has changed your life. Remind others of the forgiveness we all have in Christ. If we are trusting in Him, our sins have been paid in full. We can put off the sinful patterns of the past and put on a new character and new habits so that we act like Christ Himself (Ephesians 4:22-24; Romans 8:29).

As you remind yourself and others of these promises, you can bring hope, reduce defensiveness, make it safe to confess sin, and inspire Christ-like behavior. I've seen this principle heal deeply divided elder boards, promote respect and cooperation in the workplace, save marriages on the brink of divorce, and resolve multimillion-dollar lawsuits.

In simple terms, the more we dwell on Jesus and His gospel, the more we will reflect Jesus and His gospel, and the more our relationships will draw others near to Him.

3. Remember the Golden Result

We all know the Golden Rule: "Do to others as you would have them do to you." But do you know the Golden Result? It's a direct corollary to the Golden Rule: "Other people will usually treat you the way you treat them." Not always, but usually. Because that's how God wired us.

Blame others and they will usually blame you. Admit where you've been wrong, and you'll be surprised how often others do the same. Listen patiently and openly to others, and hold off on making premature judgments. Others will be inclined to do the same with you, which will open the way for understanding and increase the likelihood of agreement.

So anytime you're in conflict or simply want to deepen a relationship, ask yourself, "How do I want to be treated?" Then engage others by treating them exactly the same way (Matthew 7:12). You'll be amazed at how often this changes the course of a conflict and strengthens a relationship.

4. Conquer the Idols that Weaken Relationships

James 4:1 provides a key insight on conflict: "What causes quarrels and what causes fights among you? Is it not this, that your passions are at war within you?"

Many of the passions that undermine our relationships and trigger conflict are not inherently sinful. They are often good things we want too much: respect, understanding, peace and quiet, recognition of a personal sacrifice or a job well done. But good desires can still poison relationships through a downward spiral that I often refer to as the "progression of an idol:" a *good desire* turns into a *consuming demand* that leads us to *judge others* and eventually *punish* them if they don't give us what we want.

Therefore, one of the key steps in strengthening relationships and preventing or resolving conflict is to identify the desires that can trigger this progression, confess them to God, and look to Him to be the chief source of our happiness and security.

5. Guard Against "Amygdala Hijacking" in Yourself and Others

The Apostle Peter's denial of Christ is a classic example of a neurological/emotional failure that today is commonly referred to as "amygdala hijacking." As Peter demonstrates all too painfully when he denied Christ and then immediately wept with regret (Luke 22:54-62), this process typically involves sudden, intense emotions that trigger an impulsive reaction that is deeply regretted.

Most of us have experienced these types of impulsive reactions in our marriages, as well as with our children, friends, coworkers, or fellow church members.

The good news is that the Bible describes four simple steps you can follow to avoid this destructive dynamic and to take control of intense emotions. This process is summarized in the simple acrostic **READ** (**R**ecognize and name your emotions; **E**valuate their source; **A**nticipate the consequences of following them; and **D**irect the power of your emotions on a constructive course).

This simple four-step habit will enable you to harness the power of your emotions by helping your neocortex, the reasoning part of your brain, to engage quickly and effectively with your limbic system, the emotional part of your brain, so that your words and actions are thoughtful and constructive instead impulsive and hurtful.

For a detailed explanation of both the neurology and theology behind amygdala hijacking, and for two videos illustrating how the **READ** concept can be applied in daily life, see "Four Ways to Defeat Amygdala Hijacking."[3]

6. Weave Relational Wisdom into Your Life

When we face relational tensions, most of us have a tendency to go "two-dimensional." We focus obsessively on our own righteousness and the other person's wrongs. Back and forth, back and forth, and the relationship goes downhill.

Relational wisdom, which is a gospel-driven form of emotional intelligence, helps people to always view their relationships "three-dimensionally" by seeking

to be *God-aware, self-aware,* and *other-aware* in every relational interaction. Jesus taught this when He commanded us to love God with all our hearts and to love our neighbors as we love ourselves (Matthew 22:37-40).

One of the easiest ways to develop your relational wisdom is to practice four simple acrostics until these key skills become automatic habits.

Practice the SOG Plan

- Self-aware: How am I feeling and acting?
- Other-aware: How are others feeling? How am I affecting them?
- God-aware: What is God up to?

Follow a Trustworthy GPS (God-Positioning System)

- Glorify God (Trust Him absolutely)
- Pursue God (Seek Him earnestly)
- Serve God (Do what pleases Him)

READ Yourself Accurately

- Recognize and name your emotions
- Evaluate their source
- Anticipate the consequences of following them
- Direct them on a constructive course

SERVE Every Person You Meet

- Smile (Home, office, church, store, telephone)
- Explore and empathize (Show interest and compassion)
- Reconcile (Be a peacemaker)

- Value (Express appreciation and admiration)
- Encourage (Give courage, inspire, put wind under their wings)

7. Communicate So Clearly that You Cannot Be Misunderstood

Many relational tensions are triggered or inflamed by poor communication. We know what we intend to communicate, but we don't take the time to carefully evaluate and adjust our words so that they cannot be misconstrued.

As one of my mentors once taught me, "For a leader, it's not good enough to communicate so you *can be understood*. You must communicate so clearly that you *cannot be misunderstood*."

No one will get this perfect all the time, but spending a little extra time planning an email, a position paper, or an important conversation can save you many hours of unnecessary conflict.

8. Practice the Three Ps of Satisfaction

Whenever you are helping others work through relational tensions or disagreements, you are far more likely to see a positive outcome if you work diligently to provide them with the "Three Ps of Satisfaction":

- *Process satisfaction*, which requires a fair, orderly, and even-handed process where everyone feels that they've had a reasonable opportunity to present their side of the matter.

- *Personal satisfaction*, which requires treating everyone with respect, courtesy, and equality, just as we would want to be treated ourselves.

- *Product satisfaction*, which requires a final solution that is as reasonable, just, and equitable as is humanly possible.

Here's the key: Although most people involved in a decision-making or conflict-resolving process will focus their energy on achieving a particular outcome (product satisfaction), in the long run they will also place a great deal of value on how they were treated during the process. This means that even if a final decision is not entirely to their liking, they will often accept the result with equanimity if the decision-makers provided them with a high level of both process and personal satisfaction.

I cannot emphasize this point too much: Give people process satisfaction (the opportunity to fully and candidly share their views) as well as personal satisfaction (treating them with sincere courtesy and respect), and you'll be surprised how content they'll be even if they disagree with your substantive decision.

9. Constantly Build 'Passport'

Every time you engage people who are an ongoing part of your life, whether in your home, workplace, or church, you are either building or destroying "passport." A passport is an authorization to go someplace you have no inherent right to be. In relational terms, it is the permission that people give to you to enter into their lives, to learn their secrets, to know their struggles, and to offer advice and correction.

If you want other people to allow you into their lives—to have real relationship with them and to trust you to provide needed shepherding—you must earn a relational passport from every person you engage.

The best way to do so is to relate to others in such a way that they would automatically answer "yes" to three key questions:

- Can I trust you?
- Do you really care about me?
- Can you actually help me?

Each of these questions encompasses a variety of sub-questions that are always rolling around in people's minds when they are thinking of opening up to you. The more you engage people in a way that assures them that they can trust you and that you truly care about them and are able to help them, the more they will open their lives to you.[4]

10. Develop the Habit of Making Charitable Judgments

Many of the tensions and conflicts that arise in life begin or grow worse because people assume the worst about others' actions or motives. The best way for you to prevent this tendency is to ask God to help you develop the habit of making "charitable judgments" in every area of your life.

Making a charitable judgment means that out of love for God, you strive to believe the best about others until you have facts to prove otherwise. In other words, if you can reasonably interpret facts in two possible ways, God calls you to embrace the positive interpretation over the negative, or at least to postpone making any judgment at all until you can acquire conclusive facts.

To see dozens of scriptures that support this concept and several practical ways that you can apply and teach this conflict-reducing habit to your congregation, see "Charitable Judgments: An Antidote to Judging Others."[5]

11. Model Genuine Confession

At the beginning of this chapter, I described the power of the "Golden Result," the fact that other people will usually treat you the same way you treat them. This principle is especially true when you're in conflict. If you blame others for a problem, they will typically blame you right back. But if you instead confess your contribution to a problem, it's amazing how often others will follow your lead and begin to acknowledge how they have contributed to the situation as well.

When I counsel people on how to take responsibility for the way that they have contributed to a damaged relationship, I usually encourage them to make a "Seven-A Confession:"

- Address everyone involved (All those you affected)
- Avoid if, but, and maybe (Do not try to excuse your wrongs)
- Admit specifically (Both attitudes and actions)
- Acknowledge the hurt (Express sorrow for hurting someone)
- Accept the consequences (Such as making restitution)
- Alter your behavior (Change your attitudes and actions)
- Ask for forgiveness

When you take responsibility for your failures or wrongs with this kind of humility and clarity, you'll be amazed at how often the Golden Result kicks in and other people say, "Well, hold on a minute. This isn't all your fault, I admit." And then the healing begins.

12. Model Genuine Forgiveness

Many people have never seen deep, authentic forgiveness in their entire lives. Even when they hear the words, "I forgive you," they quickly learn that what those words really mean is, "I'll drop this for the moment, but I'm going to hold you at a distance emotionally for quite a while, and the next time we have a conflict, I will certainly bring this matter up again as leverage."

As a Christian, you can turn every offense into an opportunity to model a type of forgiveness that reflects the forgiveness we receive from God when we believe in the gospel. True, biblical forgiveness can be summarized with four simple promises:

- "I will not dwell on this incident."
- "I will not bring up this incident again and use it against you."
- "I will not talk to others about this incident."
- "I will not let this incident stand between us or hinder our personal relationship."

Many offenses can be quickly and easily forgiven with these simple promises. In some cases, others might be so amazed at this approach that they will say, "I've never heard of forgiveness being expressed that way. Where did you learn that?" This can lead to a conversation that eventually gives you the opportunity to explain how these promises actually reflect the forgiveness we can all receive through the gospel.

13. When You Need to Negotiate, PAUSE

Life is filled with constant negotiating, whether it involves a major business deal, competing ministry priorities, changing the family budget, or deciding where to spend this year's vacation. The Bible provides excellent guidance on how Christians can successfully negotiate the most challenging issues in life. This biblical wisdom may be summarized in an acrostic called the **PAUSE** principle of negotiating:

- **P**repare (pray, get the facts, seek godly counsel, develop options)
- **A**ffirm relationships (show genuine concern and respect for others)
- **U**nderstand interests (identify others' concerns, desires, needs, limitations, or fears)
- **S**earch for creative solutions (prayerful brainstorming)
- **E**valuate options objectively and reasonably (evaluate, don't argue)

In Philippians 2:3-4, the Apostle Paul highlighted one of the key elements of biblical negotiating when he wrote, "Do nothing out of selfish ambition or vain conceit, but in humility consider others better than yourselves. Each of you should look not only to your own interests, but also to the interests of others" (see also Matthew 22:39; 1 Corinthians 13:5; Matthew 7:12).

As you practice these simple steps over and over in your personal, work, and church negotiations, you will not only help those around you find mutually acceptable agreements, but also display a type of relational wisdom that may move others to seek your help in developing the same skills.

14. Diffuse Explosive Conversations with a Six-Part Format

Have you ever been in a family, workplace, or church meeting that was about to explode? You could feel the tension building with each person's comments and knew it was just a matter of time before the dynamite went off. Once the explosion occurs, it's often impossible to pick up the pieces.

Such explosions are not inevitable. In fact, you can turn these types of volatile engagements into an opportunity to help all of those involved participate in constructive problem-solving. The first step in this process is to summarize the issue and then ask everyone involved to commit to sharing their thoughts using a six-part format:

- Briefly stated, how do you feel because of this problem?
- What have you done that might have contributed to this problem?
- What do you think would please God as we work through this situation?
- What steps have you already taken to make things better?
- What are you now willing to do to help resolve this problem?
- What do you suggest others do to help resolve this problem?

This format can help people to become more God-aware, self-aware and other-aware by remembering God's involvement in the situation, empathizing with one another, recalling their shared frailty, getting the logs out of their own eyes, showing respect and accepting responsibility, and being solution-focused rather than attack-oriented.

15. Focus on the Good Before Itemizing the Bad

When tensions develop in our relationships, our normal tendency is to see others in an increasingly negative light, highlighting their faults and recounting their wrongs. This is a perfect strategy for weakening relationships and inflaming conflict.

Since God commands us to seek unity and reconciliation in the body of Christ, He graciously provides wisdom principles that enable us to overcome our tendency to focus on others' flaws. One of these principles is set forth in Philippians 4:8-9: "Finally, brothers, whatever is true, whatever is honorable, whatever is just, whatever is pure, whatever is lovely, whatever is commendable, if there is any excellence, if there is anything worthy of praise, think about these things."

This is one of the most effective ways to protect relationships and dampen the sparks of disagreement before they grow into a blazing conflict. When you look for and acknowledge the good in others, you see your disagreements in a more charitable light and deal with them more graciously and constructively.

And here again, the Golden Result can happen. When others hear you express respect and appreciation for their perspectives, concerns, and actions, they will often do the same toward you. And a situation that might have grown into a conflict or a broken relationship can often turn into an opportunity to strengthen a relationship and display skills that reveal Christ's work within us.

Conclusion

Most Millennials have a longing for better, deeper friendships, fewer tensions with others, greater understanding and respect, a wider circle of reliable friends and a better relationship with a spouse or significant other. The more that Christians develop and model the skills described above, the more we prove to Millennials that the church has a unique ability to satisfy their hunger for deep, authentic, and enduring relationships.

As the doors open for us to help them build these kinds of human relationships, a far more important door will also be opened—the door for the gospel of Christ to bring them into an intimate, joy-and-peace-filled relationship with their Heavenly Father.

Notes

1. George Barna, *Millennials in America* (Part I of this text), 13-14.

2. David Kinnaman, Gabe Lyons, and George Barna, *unChristian: What a New Generation Really Thinks about Christianity ... and Why It Matters* (Ada, MT: Baker Books, 2007).

3. Ken Sande, "Four Ways to Defeat Amygdala Hijacking," May 19, 2014, RW360. Available at: www.rw360.org/hijacking.

4. For more detailed guidance on developing passport, see Sande, "Three Ps of Satisfaction," May 10, 2016, RW360. Available at: www.rw360.org/3ps.

5. Sande, "Charitable Judgments: An Antidote to Judging Others," March 7, 2013, RW360. Available at: www.rw360.org/charitable.

GARRY INGRAHAM

Building Trust and Restoring Hope

Where trust has been lost, it is impossible to reestablish without truth, transparency, and authenticity. In addition, I believe a credible sense of love and genuine compassion are required for lasting trust to be securely established. Theodore Roosevelt has been quoted as saying, "No one cares how much you know, until they know how much you care." In a time when truth is considered by many to be relative ("my truth," "your truth," "my reality"), truth-thumping alone will not win hearts or minds. Truth perceived as unkind and without compassion is regarded as evil.

Without a doubt, the church has lost trust and the position of being an honorable and important spiritual institution. In fact, rather than simply being ignored by a Secular Humanist culture as prudish, ignorant, and antiquated, we seem to be rapidly moving toward a time when the church is increasingly being viewed as dangerous and hateful, in need of cancellation.

Garry Ingraham turned to Christ out of identity confusion, same-sex attraction, and sexual addiction. He later became a pastor, husband to his wife, Melissa, and father of two boys. In 2013, Garry and Melissa founded Love & Truth Network, a national, non-profit ministry focused on equipping Christian leaders to develop safe and transformational environments with the purpose of restoring sexual wholeness and biblical identity.

As I read through the results and summary found in the Millennial research by Dr. George Barna, I felt a combination of sadness for the current condition of so many Millennials, but also a great hopefulness over the possibilities a revitalized church can offer. We have an incredible opportunity to reach this generation through a renewed commitment to authenticity and lives that actually reflect a true witness of Christ-followers. Jesus has entrusted to us a message of hope and transformation, the good news of the gospel. We have an opportunity to rebuild trust out of the lack of integrity and wreckage perceived to be true (too often accurately so) about the church.

Not only do older generations need to find ways of connecting with Millennials and the generations that follow, we also have serious repenting to do in the ways we have mishandled our public and private walks with Christ.

As a kid who was born into a Christian family and grew up in church, the environment in which we lived out our Christian experience was all I knew until my mid-20s. I had no idea how unhealthy and duplicitous our Christian bubble was. My parents grew up in a similar situation. They were good and sincere people, wanting a deeper life with Christ for themselves and their children. For my father, that sincerity included a commitment of reading his Bible from cover to cover each year.

Despite sincere desire and good intentions, we were permeated by a church culture that looked good on the outside and sounded right (and to be fair, there were a lot of right things about it) but something was sick at the core. This is the church environment I grew up in, so at the time, I didn't have anything else to compare it with. Our church culture was familiar and comfortable and, to my knowledge, never questioned.

While the adults around me, especially Christian leaders, were concerned about accurate theology and well-delivered biblical teaching, it seemed that no one was paying attention to the condition of the milieu in which our theology and teaching were communicated and lived out. How were we actually doing life? What was the true condition of our hearts, our interior life? How were we applying the teachings of Scripture in our homes and families, and passing on our faith to our children and a new generation? How were we expressing the love of Christ and the fruit of the Holy Spirit? How healthy were we, actually? As it turns out, from my early Christian experience as well as countless others around my own age who have shared their experiences with me, not so much.

When I was growing up, discipleship was a class that was taught, not so much a life that was lived. I remember sitting around a table as the pastor led the "Discipleship Class." There was a lot of knowledge communicated, which was a good beginning, but very little concern for the development of wisdom, the condition of our hearts, or the practical application of the knowledge we were learning. There was no time spent in shepherding our hearts or helping us open up about our doubts and struggles with our faith—we weren't supposed to have any of those.

The topics of sex and sexuality were taboo and avoided altogether. So, we were left to ourselves to navigate and figure out this most extraordinary gift from God—the ability to create other human beings made in His image and likeness, with eternal souls. There was no discipleship on this topic when I was young. Ironically, I have learned from others 20 to 30 years younger than me that they felt like all they heard in youth group were teachings on porn and sex. But in their case, the message they received was "just don't" or "sex is bad," which ultimately led to "*you* are bad" for having sexual desires. This incredible, pleasurable, pro-creative, potentially addictive behavior, designed and intended by God for rich and free expression within the boundaries and safety of covenant marriage to produce new life and oneness of husband and wife, was poorly addressed and has become the great Achilles' heel of the church.

As a church, generally speaking, we have said many of the right things and even intellectually believed many of the right things. But the tendency toward compromise (saying one thing while doing another) has badly weakened the church and damaged our witness. Sexual sin, in particular, is a mostly hidden, stage-four cancer thriving in secrecy, darkness, and isolation in the lives of Christian men, women, youth, and even pastors and leaders within the church. We point our finger at the sexual abuse scandals of the Catholic church, but the truth is Protestant churches are full of sexual compromise and sin, including sexual abuse of children.

With easy access to and sheer abundance of pornography, Internet hook-up and cheating sites, no-fault divorce culture, accessibility of abortion, etc.,

Christians have claimed the moral high-ground while secretly self-medicating and indulging our fleshly desires just as much as the world around us.

In the words of the Apostle Paul, without biblically authentic love, we have become a noisy gong and a clanging cymbal (1 Corinthians 13:1). Double-living and hypocrisy are deep-seated issues within the Christian community. Recently, I've been reading through First and Second Kings and am sharply reminded how sexual immorality and idolatry were two primary sins that enslaved God's people over and over again. Even King Solomon, the wisest man who has ever lived and who began his reign so well in humility and ardent trust in God, failed miserably in the later years of life and reign by allowing his heart to be turned away from God toward sexual immorality and idolatry. Like the people of God in the Old Testament, our churches are full of Christians practicing sexual immorality and idolatry.

There is nothing wrong with the foundation of the church. The foundation is securely established on the unchanging and immovable rock of Jesus Christ and His finished work on the cross. However, some of the "building materials" of the church have been fashioned after human tradition and the fleshly desire of many who have gone before us (and many who are currently leading and attending) to appear far more whole and righteous than they actually were. In the words of Andrew Comiskey, founder of Desert Stream Ministries, "We care more about the *appearance* of health than actual health." [1]

The focus of our ministry efforts at Love & Truth Network[2] is always toward systemic, environmental shifts within the churches where we minister, building toward long-term connection and encouragement with church leadership. Church culture doesn't change overnight, and while solid teaching is an essential beginning, it's only that—a beginning. True and accurate teaching, based on true and accurate theology, provides the building materials we need. Yet, the question remains, how will we build? Will we build skillfully with integrity, or will we cut corners and perform shoddy work, hiding flaws behind a veneer of wholeness, strength, or beauty?

Just like the Pharisees, many of us as Christians have learned to use the Bible either as a weapon to point out the flaws in others or to superficially apply theology and biblical teaching to window-dress our own lives, cleaning the "outside of our cup" while the hidden parts of our lives—the inside—"is full of robbery and self-indulgence" (Matthew 23:25).

As I read Dr. Barna's research, these are some of the things that jumped out at me. I am reminded of a statement attributed to Mahatma Gandhi that I believe describes the attitude of many toward the church and Christianity, "I like your Christ, I do not like your Christians. Your Christians are so unlike your Christ."

I am also reminded of God's continual revelation in the Old Testament and attempts to correct His chosen people. In particular, His words written through Isaiah the prophet: "I have spread out My hands all day long to a rebellious people, who walk in the way, which is not good, following their own thoughts" (Isaiah 65:2).

Over and over again, God reveals His primary prescription for healing and His design for rich, authentic community. We read His instructions regarding a lifestyle of confession and vulnerability in James 5:16: "Therefore, confess your sins to one another, and pray for one another, that you might be healed. The effective prayer of a righteous man can accomplish much." By their lack of obedience, most Christians reject this command and choose to keep their sin struggles (especially of a sexual nature) to themselves and God alone. They cling to 1 John 1:9 "If we confess our sins, He is faithful and righteous to forgive us our sins and to cleanse us from all unrighteousness." This verse, pulled out of its communal context, makes confession a private matter, only between the individual and God.

In addition, we read God's instruction for walking in the light in 1 John 1:7: "But if we walk in the light, as He is in the light, we have fellowship with one another, and the blood of Jesus His Son cleanses us from all sin." By living in confessional isolation regarding our sins and struggles, we may have the promise of God's forgiveness in 1 John 1:9, but we bypass the true fellowship that comes from walking in the light and being fully known by at least some others within the Body of Christ. In doing this, we are depriving ourselves of the healing that is activated by confession to other trusted brothers or sisters through the prayers we offer up to God on behalf of one another, as described in James 5:16: "Therefore, confess your sins to one another, and pray for one another so that you may be healed. A prayer of a righteous person, when it is brought about, can accomplish much."

Whenever we bypass God's clearly revealed will and make our own pathway, it often appears pious and even religious, but it's empty of real life and devoid of God's power, and ultimately leads to death (Proverbs 14:12; 16:25). Given enough time, the practice (whatever it may be) becomes a familiar and sometimes imperceptible aspect of the way we live out our Christian experience.

A vital and necessary blessing of confession to one another is the death-blow it delivers to our "social saint"—that carefully crafted, polished image we constantly strive to present to everyone around us. In our flesh, most of us will do anything to avoid an experience of exposure, including full and honest confession. It requires an act of our will to reveal our sins and struggles and our ongoing need for forgiveness, grace, and a vulnerable, transparent community. In doing so, we keep in check our strong temptation to present ourselves to others as better than we actually are. Thereby, walking in the light, we receive a regular supply of empowerment and actual nourishing fellowship with God and others. The blessings that flow from these acts of humility and obedience are boundless—both to ourselves and the community around us.

Would the Millennial and younger generations be able to articulate all this about the church? Unlikely, but they have a very keen sense for the inauthentic, and their radar for hypocrisy has picked up on the double-speak and double-living permeating the church. Paul warns in 2 Timothy 3:5: "Holding to a form of godliness, although they have denied its power; avoid such men as these."

From my perspective, the general negative critique of the church by the unchurched is quite often legitimate—at least in part. But the solutions offered by the world miss the mark of God altogether. Historically, the church has had two broad responses. One response is to hunker down, dig our heels in, and use truth as a weapon and religious rhetoric as way to point out other people's brokenness, driving them away from Christ and His church. The other response tends to be capitulation and surrender to the world; a reduction of biblical truth so as not to offend anyone, thereby removing the full reality of our sin, our need for repentance, our desperate need for a savior, our utterly wretched and lost condition without Him, and ultimately, our need to surrender to the Lordship of Christ. Many Sunday morning messages are more reminiscent of an informative and well-crafted TED Talk than preaching and teaching the truths of God's Word.

To rebuild trust and restore hope, we as Christ-followers must live an authentic life of discipleship. Jesus calls His followers to a narrow way, rather than the wide path chosen by most (Matthew 7:13-14). Jesus exhorts us to the practice of denying ourselves (our fleshly desires) by taking up our cross (death to self) and following after Him (Matthew 16:24).

Through His finished work on the cross, we are invited to become sons and daughters of God. We are invited into a new and eternal family. Dr. Barna's research confirms that Millennials are searching for a sense of belonging. They need relationships that are deep and real. Yet a sense of meaningful purpose eludes them. They are often looking in all the wrong places, having written off Christianity and the church as irrelevant to their lives, and perhaps an evil institution altogether, but they are searching, nonetheless. Their hearts and minds are fertile ground for the authentic Gospel of Jesus, lived out through an authentic, warm, and truthful witness of His church.

As Christ-followers, we have an opportunity to turn the ship around, beginning with repentance from our "good false-selves" that we have erected for others to see and value. We must consistently move forward living a lifestyle of authentic and intentional vulnerability and the practice of confession to our inner circle (our band of brothers or sisters). We have an opportunity to restore the Church as a shining light on a hill—a beacon of hope, a hospital for healing.

We need to become ruthless in tearing down our personal, modern-day idols and purge God's house of the hypocrisy thriving within. It is amazing that Christians can read Jesus' sharp rebuke of the religious leaders and Pharisees, calling out their double standard and double-living, exposing them for their well-manicured, outer appearance, while their insides are full of rot and death, but totally miss the fact that His words apply to us today.

2 Kings 22 records the life of Josiah, a boy who became king over Judah at only eight years of age. He succeeded two wicked kings who "seduced them to do evil more than the nations whom the Lord destroyed before the sons of Israel" (2 Kings 21:9). However, Josiah's heart was totally committed to

the LORD his God: "Nor did he turn aside to the right or to the left" (2 Kings 22:2).

Over the course of the dark history of Judah, there were a few good kings who followed God throughout their reign, but often they made compromises or ignored the high places where the people worshiped false gods, along with Yahweh. But Josiah was exceptional. He tore down and destroyed every idol and purged every place where false gods were worshiped.

In addition, the house of God had been neglected and in great need of repair. Josiah set the workmen to this task. God is always with and for those who practice truth and humble themselves before Him, seeking Him and His ways with all their heart. In fact, 2 Kings 23:25 states about Josiah: "Before him there was no king like him who turned to the LORD with all his heart and with all his soul and with all his might, according to all the law of Moses; nor did any like him arise after him."

We're in desperate need of some Josiahs today. We need Josiahs leading churches, leading businesses, leading in political office, and leading, working, and ministering in all walks of life. Of course, it isn't only about leaders. We also need followers. We hear a lot about leadership and very little about follower-ship. We need clear-eyed, strong, bold, compassionate, gracious men and women who live out and embody what it means to "love God with all their heart, soul, and mind" (Matthew 22:37) as leaders and followers.

In addition to Josiah's incredible example of tearing down what is unholy to rebuild that which is holy and God-honoring, we have the simple, brief statement in 1 Chronicles 12:32 about the sons of Issachar, described as "men who understood the times, with knowledge of what Israel should do." As the Millennial research is read and carefully considered, we need men and women within the Church like the sons of Issachar.

Having served on a pastoral staff team for 12 years and now working with and equipping various pastors, teams, and churches around the nation, I spend time with many wonderful churches whose leaders pour out their lives to serve and lead those in their care. However, with regard to the true needs of Millennials revealed in the Barna research (as well as younger generations), I'm rarely finding pastors or leaders who both understand the times and have clear direction and knowledge of what they and their church can and should do.

I believe every church should have a sensitivity to seekers. I wish every Christian church had a growth track toward becoming a "teaching hospital" for the recovery and healing of the spiritually and emotionally struggling and ill. If not, what are we doing? What is our purpose? How are we fulfilling the Great Commission in our own community and city? If not, we run the risk of becoming an ingrown and irrelevant group of people, adding to the negative perspective of the unchurched against Christianity.

The "seeker-sensitive" or "emerging church" movements were birthed out of an admirable motivation to reach unchurched people with the gospel of Jesus Christ. While many church leaders became enamored with the methods espoused by these movements (I attended several Willow Creek leadership summits with a dozen other pastors and elders from my church), we see decades later the outcomes of these movements have actually led to a watered-down version of the gospel and often shallow discipleship.

Over the course of time, in the pursuit of becoming "attractional" and popular, these churches not only created an inviting atmosphere but also softened and modified their message. It was such a gradual shift, the changes were nearly imperceptible. Much of the language remained the same—gospel, grace, love, following Jesus, etc., while other words and phrases like sin, Hell, repentance, surrender, dying to self, lordship of Christ, etc., became more and more scarce until they were never mentioned again.

It seems these churches were like the proverbial frog in the pot of water, heated ever so slowly the frog didn't perceive its demise. These churches often grew very quickly and sometimes to a massive size. Willow Creek Community Church is one of the most notable mega-churches that embraced and fostered the hyper-seeker-sensitive movement. They grew in size, but often lacked in depth and discipleship.

Of course, I believe there's value in churches pursuing excellence and an inviting, impactful Sunday morning encounter with God. And that His people, seekers and regular attenders alike, experience God through relational connections and touch-points, fun and safe environments (especially for children), genuine worship, use of technology, the message, and every other possible detail. As long as a desired positive experience doesn't come at the expense of clearly communicated and oftentimes hard-hitting truth—divine truth that has the power to change lives. Not because we are trying to make the scriptures hard-hitting, but because we aren't skipping difficult passages or softening the text to remove all possible discomfort.

More than a decade ago a pastor friend of mine and I were having this very discussion about how it seemed that even many churches calling themselves evangelical were actually watering down the gospel in an attempt to get people in the door and then get them to return. It seemed like a "bait and switch," which would have been bad enough, but too often the "switch" never happens. Rather, the church tends to slide further toward what is now called "progressive." Given the fact that Jesus has some pretty harsh words for the churches of Revelation 2 and 3 and their various forms of compromise—often sexual and idolatrous compromises—a more apt term for what is called the "progressive" church would be better labeled as the "regressive" church. My friend made a statement that day I have never forgotten and often repeat, "What we win them with is what we win them to."

From my two decades of full-time pastoral and ministry work, I believe younger generations long to be "called up in love." I was talking with a pastor of pastors recently. He's often invited into settings where Millennial pastors and young Christian leaders are the majority in the room. When he asks them their greatest need as a Christian and Christian leader, the one answer far and above any other is "mentoring." They want an older person in the faith to care about them, to love them, to listen to them, to offer guidance, and to walk with them.

We don't often think about the fact that many (perhaps most) young Christian leaders have not been fathered well, or at all. They are struggling as young single men or women—do they have what it takes? What can they do about the gnawing questions, fears, and void in their hearts—who can they tell? They are struggling in their marriages, struggling with lust and porn, struggling to self-medicate their inner pain in some other way. Once they enter ministry, the stakes are even higher to keep up an appearance of having it all together. But they don't have it all together—far from it. So, they cast a competent and confident image, while actually leading out compromise and duplicity until they implode through burnout, a sex scandal, a marriage that falls apart, or some other way.

I had the privilege of serving on a pastoral team at a local church a number of years ago. At one point we recognized that we needed coaching in how to shepherd our large youth ministry well. We searched and interviewed consultant organizations with expertise in working with youth. We made a decision and began a lengthy process, which included interviews with young people, parents, youth workers, staff, and pastors. After many months, the pastoral staff sat down with this organization to hash through the report they developed based upon their experience, expertise, interactions, and interviews with many in our church. It was all very informative and helpful in guiding our decisions and direction. But the truth is, I can't remember anything about the specifics of their input or recommendations, with the exception of one statement.

I was shocked when I heard the youth consultant correct an assumption one of us expressed. He said, "Actually, we have found over and over again that a young person is drawn to the oldest person in the room who will give them the time of day." Is that really true? I wondered. Many years later, I believe it is. Just as fathers and mothers are responsible for taking initiative to build relationship with their sons and daughters (not the other way around), older "fathers" and "mothers" in the faith should be seeking God and keeping their eyes open for those He would bring to them for care, guidance, and growth in their faith—in other words, discipleship.

I believe we, as redeemed sons and daughters of God, need to participate in a dramatic shift in the typical culture of nearly every local church body. We need to live out God's commands to step out of our darkness and shadows and walk in the light (1 John 1:7). We need to embrace a lifestyle of confession. We need to make it a priority to seek and invite a small band of brothers or sisters around us for the mutual benefit, encouragement, and building up of all. We need to offer our lives and homes (of which we are stewards, not owners) as instruments to fulfill God's heart communicated in Psalm 68:6: "God takes the lonely and puts them in family." Re-read and ponder that statement for a moment before reading on. Might you and your family or your home be part of the answer to someone's loneliness and ultimate spiritual and emotional growth? Is there someone God wants to put into His family by placing them with you and your family?

Psalm 68:6 continues: "Only the rebellious dwell in a parched land." Since individualism is ingrained in our American culture, there are plenty of people who will choose to live alone. But there are many whose hearts long for family. This was true of me, especially when Jesus was journeying with me out of LGBTQ+ identity and behavior. In my repentance of sin and surrender to the lordship of Jesus, I needed more than a Sunday morning experience and a mid-week Bible study (as much as those were important and necessary). I needed more than an occasional dinner with a family in the church. I needed to be in family. I needed a healthy environment where I was loved and wanted. I needed a place where I could see and experience imperfect people living out an authentic walk with Jesus and with one another. I needed a place to belong and a place for my soul to heal and grow as a man and a son.

As I read the *Millennials in America* report, I am full of hope that God isn't merely calling the church to figure out a new approach to attract Millennials and younger generations. We've tried that and failed. God isn't just calling us to do a better job of helping the "poor young people who are lost 'out there' in the world." Rather, in Jesus' love for His bride, I believe He is using this research from Dr. Barna as a wake-up call to us, His church.

I am reminded of the seventh and final church Jesus addresses in Revelation 2 and 3, the church in Laodicea. He is very sharp in His rebuke of the church, which so resembles the current condition of our American churches. It would be worth meditating on and spending some time in Revelation 3:14-22, but here I want to highlight verse 18:

> I advise you to buy from Me gold refined by fire so that you may become rich, and white garments so that you may clothe yourself, and that the shame of your nakedness will not be revealed; and eye salve to anoint your eyes so that you may see.

It's that eye-salve statement that comes to mind as I finish. We need God's eye salve to see our way forward clearly—to move into our own personal repentance and corporate repentance, toward renewed purpose, vitality, and life.

God isn't calling us to find and implement some flashy and appealing new method. We can ditch the new fog machine, the latest cool (and unnecessary) tech gadget, and the 40-something pastor trying to be cool. God is calling us to authentic, integrated, vulnerable, integrous lives—lived out in radical love, truth, and sacrificial community.

Notes

1. According to the Desert Streams Ministries website, Andrew Comiskey founded Desert Streams and Living Water Ministries, when he as his wife, Annette, responded to their pastor's call to start a healing / support group in West Hollywood, California, for men and women seeking Jesus in light of unwanted same-sex attraction. Accessed at: https://desertstream.org/.

2. More information about the ministry of Love & Truth Network is available at: https://loveandtruthnetwork.com/.

DR. JOHN JACKSON

Millennials in America: Weeping Now and Joy is Coming!

We may weep through the night, but at daybreak it will turn into shouts of ecstatic joy—Psalm 30:5 (The Passion Translation)

My first few reactions to the report, *Millennials in America: New Insights into the Generation of Growing Influence*,[1] were entirely emotional (weeping) and negative (despairing). But the more I read and prayed over the report, the more positive and hope-filled I became. That journey of emotional and mental response is a picture of what I think the report says. First readings of the report might lead you to a singularly negative conclusion, but I personally believe the opposite after a second and third reading. The report contains sobering details to be sure and is a cause for strong consideration and accountability. The crisis many have felt or will feel when reading this research is understandable. Yet I find signs of hope in the research and believe we are heading toward joy in the morning!

John Jackson, Ph.D., is the President of William Jessup University (www.jessup. edu) and is the author of nine books on leadership and transformation (additional information at www. drjohnjackson.com), including the new book, Grace Ambassador: Bringing Heaven on Earth *(Chosen Books, 2023). Dr. Jackson and his wife, Pam, make their home in Northern California.*

I'm grateful for George Barna and his decades-long work on U.S. patterns of religious behavior and beliefs. I'm also thankful for my friends Len Munsil and Tracy Munsil at Arizona Christian University (ACU) and the Cultural Research Center at ACU, along with my friend Dave Dias of Foundations of Freedom, who commissioned the research. I personally read many of Dr. Barna's books and reports before having the occasion to speak at an event with him many years ago, and that experience stuck with me. We've had occasional but limited contact since then, and the occasion of this report has been a happy reconnection for me. Dr. Barna has been measuring biblical worldview prevalence and factors since at least the early 1990s. His long history with this subject helps us to normalize this survey with others he has conducted throughout his illustrious career.

One of the reasons that weeping was my first reaction and despair my second is that I have spent the vast majority of my professional life in pastoral and leadership ministry in the Body of Christ. Though I'm on the "young" side of the Boomer generation, I have spent my entire life encapsulated in the Boomer experience. My generation's characteristics and biases are well known and chronicled in our culture through written and video narratives. From my particular perspective, the journey of the local church and leadership during this season is worthy of particularly humble and self-critical awareness. Sadly, from my standpoint, we have pastored and led the generation known as Millennials and the cultural results of our labors are not good. We must be accountable for them as they happened on our watch. My friends Samuel Rodriguez and Dr. Ché Ahn reflect this need for humility and repentance in their contributions to this volume. Not only do I concur with them in that regard, but I have also had many moments of repentance before the Lord and before His people, as we recognize that we have collectively missed the mark of faithfulness in some significant ways.

The statistics and self-perceptions of Millennials we read about in this research have taken place on our cultural watch.

All the while, we have had large and growing churches and have been self-congratulatory regarding our success. But the research now shows we have seen a generation grow more uncertain and unclear about the purpose of life and more despondent about the values and meaning of relationships and social structures. My initial despair over these findings was not an irrational response:

- Nearly three-fourths of Millennials describe their lives as having no purpose.
- Millennials have the highest suicide rate of any generation previously studied.
- Millennials highly value relationships, but fewer than four out of 10 believe they have quality intimate relationships.
- 80% of Millennials do not believe that life is sacred and do not practice the Golden Rule ("Do unto others as you would have them do unto you").
- Over half of Millennials frequently struggle with anxiety, depression, and fear.
- 40% of Millennials do not believe God exists.
- 4% of Millennials—and only 2% of the youngest Millennials—have a biblical worldview.[2]

These are sobering realities. And these beliefs are being manifested in our current cultural malaise as we experience the aftereffects of these belief and value statements. In my own work with Millennials at my university campus, I sense that many of them grapple with the pressure to adopt the increasingly prevalent and forceful false narratives that are pervasive in social and traditional media. The Millennial Generation and the one that follows (Gen Z) are experiencing corrosive and widespread mental, emotional, and social pressures. The tepid and crumbling response of the generations to that pressure demonstrates the clear lack of an unequivocal and compelling biblical worldview in the vast majority of Millennials.

Millennials without a biblical worldview who are absorbing the previously unknown reality of constant "message pressure" from their multiple social media platforms are systematically susceptible to a sense of disequilibrium across culture. For the generations that follow, and for those of us who continue in positions of influence and spiritual direction, this research is a compelling and clarion call for Christian education—a call to Christ-centered, biblically grounded discipleship education that recovers the essential linkage between family, church, and school.

To be frank, my first priority is not the university (although I have huge concerns there; a previous work of mine, *The Right Choice*,[3] gives some foundational guidance to that particular decision process). My priorities are the family and then the church. As a fundamental matter, I do want to note that I have many concerns about the nature of higher education in America, including private faith-based higher education. Most important of my concerns is the spiritually animating force of what has become of public higher education in America. I believe that much of higher education today is designed with an intent to "deconstruct" the worldview and cultural values of incoming students. They then "reconstruct" in some presumed pathway of enlightenment that often occurs with the guidance of a professorial class which has intended from the beginning to destroy the foundations of faith, family, and freedom in our country.

Many parents assume, having understood at least in general terms the destructive pathway of the typical higher education system, that they can protect their student by sending them to a faith-based university. Sadly, many historically faith-based universities have more in common with their public counterparts than their faith history. Students in these schools often leave their faith and family with similar brokenness upon graduation. Parents and students must educate themselves before they enter their college experience.[4]

Assuming alignment of values between family, church, and school is a dangerous practice in our day.

Vigilance from dads and moms in every arena of life, but particularly in the educational and media realms, is critical. I believe that education and media have been the two most pernicious agents in the attack against the foundational values of our nation and community in the six decades of my life.

These last decades have demonstrated an almost complete and systematically brutal, effective attack upon the institution of the family in American culture. I am heartbroken about the incidence of fatherless households, childless households by choice, and the incidence of divorce and cohabitation in our nation. In the midst of all this, where have we been as the church? Yes, I pastored and led churches and a denominational unit from the late 1980s through the early 2010s, and I bear specific responsibility for failings in my own leadership. To the extent that my leadership was deficient, I humbly repent and find rest in the goodness of God (Romans 2:4).

I believe that the attacks on marriage, family, sexuality, and gender identity are highly weaponized tools of the enemy of our soul. Pain and sorrow have been the inheritance of a society that walks away from the biblical building blocks of any successful civilization. I am committed to biblical views of gender, sexuality, marriage, and family where parents have the right and responsibility to protect children from harmful decisions and input. Often when Christians advocate for these positions, they are seen as longing for a return to a hazy version of the 1950s. That is not true. Christians are advocating for what God has designed as best. I'm praying with some specific targets in my heart:

> I believe in and am staking the rest of my life on this planet on the belief that Jesus' people can be discipled and equipped by the five-fold ministry (engaging the spiritual gifts described in Ephesians 4:12) and that they can then become reproducing disciple makers who live in society for the glory of God.

> I see a church engaged in society, with redemptive love and full of grace and truth, contending for what heaven on earth looks like in the critical issues of our day.

> I see assemblies of believers in all 3,000 counties of the United States living for the glory of God and following Jesus with radical love, radical truth, and radical grace.

> I see the church living fully armored and recognizing that we are not in a country club, we are not called to survive the prison camp until we get rescued, but we are called to defeat the enemy in a very real war (Ephesians 6).

> I see the church that Jesus loves, loving the world that Jesus died for and living for the Kingdom that Jesus ushered in to our planet.

> I see the Savior, His Bride, His Kingdom, and His will being done "on earth, as it is in heaven" (Matthew 6:10).

That is the church I see and the world I am called to contend for.

In the midst of it all, what has the church done to build strong families? Are we equipping children to grow up and become fathers and mothers who raise up more children to be fathers and mothers (1 John 2)? Many families that exist today have never experienced the love of a healthy father or mother. The opportunity to create healthy families by modeling and mentoring is singularly one of the greatest opportunities for the church today. If every church community were to build strong family units, I believe the health of the church and culture in America would be vastly different from what we are now experiencing. I am likewise convinced that much of what we have done in the church these past few decades has been more accommodating to the culture rather than redemptively affecting the culture as "salt and light" (Matthew 5).

The fundamental mission of the church is to live to the praise and glory of God (Ephesians 1) by being ambassadors of reconciliation (2 Corinthians 5) in the world and disciple nations (Matthew 28) through the equipping of the saints by the five-fold ministry leaders (apostles, prophets, evangelists, pastors, and teachers described in Ephesians 4). I am believing for Jesus' prayer in Matthew 6:10, "On earth as it is in heaven." I'm 61 and have lived a pretty decent amount of time on this planet, and to be frank, I'm not sure we have really experienced "Heaven on Earth" much these days.

In Matthew 16:18, Peter makes his confession of Christ and Jesus declares that the gates of hell will not prevail against the church. Look around us. Why is the church not prevailing? The church has actually been retreating against the giants of culture. Instead of coming out against the giants in the name of the Lord as young David did, we have been retreating. Why has the church retreated? Join me as we press in to hear the Spirit's call to the prevailing church that is emerging like a shepherd boy from the crowd.

One more generation of "convenience Christianity" will sow more destructive seeds for Millennials and Gen Z. We have to live redemptively, connecting salvation and sanctification in an organic and life-giving fashion that is full of the Word and full of the Spirit. Living in such a way that our personal encounter with Jesus is a vibrant and animating daily reality equips us to then engage the culture around us in personal relationships, in our workplace, and in the public square. As my friend Samuel Rodriguez often says, our engagement in the public square must be about righteousness and redemption with the "Agenda of the Lamb and not the donkey or the elephant." Engagement in the public square is fundamentally about the Great Commission and not about politics.[5]

Author Os Guinness is prescient on these matters, as always:

> In short, the decisive power is always God's, through his Word and Spirit. But on her side the church contributes three distinct human factors to the equation: engagement, discernment, and refusal. First, the church is called to engage and to stay engaged, to be faithful and obedient in that it puts aside all other preferences of its own and engages purposefully with the world as its Lord commands. Second, the church is called to discern, to exercise its spiritual and cultural discernment of the best and worst of the world of its day, in order to see clearly where it is to be "in" and where it is to be "not of" that world. And third, the church is called to refuse, a grand refusal to conform to or comply with anything and everything in the world that is against the way of Jesus and his kingdom.[6]

So then, what are we to make of this report and wherein does our hope lie? I believe the *Millennials in America* report is a clarion call for families, the church, and schools to make biblical worldview an anchoring reality in our daily lives. The research is challenging to be sure, but there are the seeds of hope that call out from its pages for us to have a redemptive passion to reach the Millennial Generation. In fact, the more I read the report, the more I was encouraged! My spirit began to be lifted as I felt like the Lord was saying to me, "This is not a generation lost. This is a generation desperately wanting to be found." A full 75% of Millennials are looking for purpose in life![7] What an amazing, historic opportunity.

Millennials are looking for meaning and purpose. But it is equally clear that they are famished for nourishing relationships of depth and connection. If the Body of Christ is to see this as our redemptive moment, it is clear that we need relationships with Millennials with lots of truth in love. In my experience in the church and in my own life, often there are times I love to give truth, but there's not much love given with it. So, we need a lot of truth in love. We need to create safe places (not these safety zones where people cannot talk about differences without being "harmed") where Millennials know they are loved. And we can encourage them to ask questions. For those of us who are Boomers, we simply must find a Millennial leader or two (or three), invest in them, love them, support them, and strengthen them. We also need to pray for God to lift up Joshuas from the Millennial generation. We need to be and create leaders who traffic in hope. It is true that my first responses to this research were weeping and despairing. But I kept feeling like the Spirit was telling me: "Look, you're leading a college, you're leading a university. You have the opportunity as a pastor, as a business leader, as a K-12 leader, to speak hope into this generation." And so, I want us Builders, Boomers, and Xer's to be people of hope and be the most pro-Millennial generations we can be. This is our opportunity. This is not simply devastating news in this research. It's a wake-up call—and an opportunity to be people of hope.

Dr. Barna and the leadership of Arizona Christian University and its Cultural Research Center have actually given us a profound gift. The "alarm-clock" experience of our first exposure to the research should not cause us to remain in shock and immobilized. Rather, we hear the alarm—and we respond.

I choose to think of our times as framed by the 9/11 experience. Do you remember when you first saw the horrifying images of the planes hitting the towers and even seeing some people jump to their deaths from the upper stories rather than be consumed by fire? Do you remember the masses running from the impact zone to get away from the burning buildings and the horror of the impact? But do you also remember seeing the images of the firefighters and other first responders running into the buildings? Of the 2,977 people who died on 9/11, 414 of them were first responders on the ground in New York City who ran toward the crisis rather than away from it. And just as on 9/11, those 414 gave their lives for rescue, I believe the Lord is going to raise up a multitude of rescuers as we run toward the crisis rather than away from it. I think the "fields are white unto harvest" (John 4:35) and this is our moment to run into the fields! It is "go time!"

This research that comes shrouded as a crisis is actually coming in a moment of profound meaning and opportunity for the people of God. I'm convinced that we were made for such a time as this. I'm convinced that the people of God are ready and have what it takes to bring life and freedom to a generation that might believe its future is dark, and without meaning or depth of relationships.

A Second Reformation Declaration for Our Time

These are times that provide opportunity for family and church and community to experience the presence of God in new dimensions of faith and encounter. The people of God assembled together in communities of faith for worship, teaching, fellowship, ministry, and evangelism is a powerful manifestation of His life in community. Now, as much as ever, we desperately need the church to be released into the world, to be "salt and light" for the glory of Jesus.

We are believing for a prevailing church. On the authority of the words of Jesus and in the power of His resurrection, I am declaring that the era of a passive, weak, disengaged, fear-filled church is over. The people of God are waking up, rising up, and being stirred up for battle against the enemy. Though he is indeed a thief (John 10:10) and prowls like a lion (1 Peter 5:8), we declare that the only lion who matters is the Lion of the tribe of Judah, and Jesus is His name (Isaiah 11:6, Revelation 5).

We want to see an explosion of "grace distributed" in every sphere of society. I'm dreaming of the church being a discipling and equipping center, as it incarnates what Ephesians 4 describes as the "equipping of the saints for the work of ministry." I believe for, see, and want to multiply Christ-followers in business, education, government, arts and media, family, and church all testifying to a transformational relationship and experience with Jesus Christ.

We are living in a time of serious cultural giants: historical revisionism, abortion and euthanasia, religious repression, racism and injustice, as well as redefined identity and family. We believe God is calling His people to establish a clear and compelling framework for revival and reformation in our time. And just like David's stones, these are the "5 Smooth Stones" that will slay the giants of our time:

5 Smooth Stones for the Church in Culture:

- **Foundations:** We are committed to biblical authority in life and view our Constitution as a stewardship trust so that we can see our nation bring glory to God through our national character.

- **Life:** We are committed to treating all human life as precious and made in the image of God. We honor life in the womb and outside the womb until natural death.

- **Liberty:** We are committed to religious and economic liberty, and believe that a socialist economic and political system is the greatest natural threat to liberty around the world.

- **Justice:** We are committed to a biblical experience of racial unity, justice, and application of a biblical experience full of grace and truth to reforming our healthcare, immigration, and criminal justice systems.

- **Family:** We are committed to biblical views of gender, sexuality, marriage, and family where parents have the right and responsibility to protect children from harmful decisions and inputs.

During the early days of COVID, I felt a particularly strong urging and wrote a short little book called, *The Prevailing Church: Confronting the Five Giants of Culture*. In the midst of that, I called forth what I believe about these moments. I am not afraid of these days—I am energized by them! I believe we are standing on the edge of what I have been calling a "Second Reformation." I see that Second Reformation has been in the birthing canal for the past two or three decades. I offer this declaration for your consideration. We have been weeping, but the joy that is our inheritance is a "right now" word! Let us go forth in the power of the Holy Spirit and in the presence of Jesus as we magnify the name of the Lord and claim each generation as a people for His glory.

Notes

1. For a more complete treatment, see: John Jackson, *The Prevailing Church: Confronting the Five Giants of Culture* (Rocklin, CA: Jessup University Press, 2021).

2. George Barna, *Millennials in America: New Insights into the Generation of Growing Influence*, Cultural Research Center at Arizona Christian University, commissioned by Foundations of Freedom (November 2021). The full research report is included as Part 1 of this text.

3. Barna, *Millennials in America* (Part 1 of this text), 24-27.

4. John Jackson, *The Right Choice: Choosing a College and Why It Matters* (Rocklin, CA: Jessup University Press, 2019).

5. A number of excellent resources exist for guiding the college decision, including my short book, *The Right Choice*. Also see: Len Munsil, *Transforming Culture with Truth* (Glendale, AZ, Arizona Christian University Press, 2020) and Everett Piper, *Not a Day Care: The Devastating Consequences of Abandoning Truth* (Irving, TX: Salem Books, 2017).

6. See Samuel Rodriguez's contribution to this text, "Restoring Millennials with the Agenda of the Lamb," 121-131.

7. Os Guinness, *Renaissance: The Power of the Gospel No Matter How Dark the Times* (Westmont, IL: InterVarsity Press, 2017), 84-85.

8. Barna, *Millennials in America*, 26.

JEFF PHILLIPS

Helping Millennials Through Authentic, Purpose-Driven Community

As I read Dr. Barna's *Millennials in America* report, I see two specific data points that, at first, appear to reflect dissonance within the minds of Millennials. On one hand, the research shows that Millennials embrace Postmodernism mixed with a syncretistic mashup of elements from other worldviews, including Nihilism, Secular Humanism, Marxism, and Eastern Mysticism.[1]

A key tenet of both Postmodernism and Nihilism is the rejection of any overarching metanarratives that make sense of the world and provide a cohesive accounting of human history. On the other hand, 75% of Millennials indicate their "desire to identify a purpose for living,"[2] which presupposes the possibility of a metanarrative at some level of existence. I wondered

Jeff Phillips is assistant professor of biblical and theological studies at Arizona Christian University. He holds a Master of Divinity and is currently pursuing a Doctorate in New Testament Studies. Before coming to ACU, Jeff served 12 years as a campus evangelist. During that time, he helped plant two churches, one in New Zealand and one in Tampa, Florida. Jeff and his wife, Lisa, have four children, the oldest of whom is a sophomore at ACU.

what could explain this clear disconnect within Millennials—the conceptual rejection of metanarratives (especially on a cosmic scale), yet a deep desire for a grand story in their personal lives.

York Moore, national evangelist for InterVarsity Christian Fellowship USA, argues that Millennials have not rejected metanarratives per se, but are hungry for a new metanarrative.[3] As I contemplated Moore's assertion in light of Dr. Barna's research, it occurred to me that instead of a carte blanche rejection of all grand narratives, Millennials may be reacting against a particular metanarrative that has pervaded modern American Christianity.

This grand narrative is the overly individualized presentation of the Gospel—namely, the presentation of the Gospel that goes something like this: *"You* are a sinner deserving of eternal punishment, but Christ died for *you* so that *you* can go to heaven when *you* die." Certainly, this is a fundamental and essential element of the gospel, but it does not capture *all* that God will achieve in redemption. We know from the biblical witness that God's intention is to renew all that He has made (Romans 8:18-23; Revelation 21:5), Or as N.T. Wright puts it, "[U]ltimately, all creation will be set right."[4] And most exciting, God wants to involve us in His project of reclamation.

Whether fairly or unfairly, recent generations (including Millennials) have judged the church's over-individualized presentation of the Gospel more as a condemnation of their sinful lifestyles by holier-than-thou preachers, who all too often have been exposed as hypocrites, than as a life-giving offer of grace. As Dr. JoAnna Dias noted during the second Millennial Panel, "[Millennials] are disillusioned with the church. ... The people that they see in their lives aren't living biblically; they aren't living authentically."[5] Dr. Barna also speaks of the importance of authenticity for this generation.[6]

The vast majority of Millennials desire to find purpose for their lives and want authentic relationships. In nearly 27 years working with college students, my experiences affirm the truth of these points from Dr. Barna's research.

After graduating college in the mid-1990s, I joined my church's ministry staff as a campus evangelist working full-time to reach college students with the Gospel and then to disciple them to be followers of Jesus Christ. During those 15 years, the oldest of the Millennial generation began attending college. My wife was also a campus evangelist. We were privileged to work with many hundreds of students over the years, first at the University of Arizona in Tucson, then in two university-based church plants in New Zealand and Tampa, Florida, and finally at Arizona State University, while I earned my Master of Divinity at Phoenix Seminary. We saw firsthand that young people—especially Millennials—are attracted to vibrant, purpose-driven community.

Our church's evangelism staff organized and hosted dynamic fellowship activities, both on campus (in dorms, fraternity and sorority houses, and various university venues) and off-campus in private homes, and public venues (such as sports complexes, bowling alleys, and entertainment venues). Private donors pitched in to provide free food and activities. Our ministry strategically planned multiple events as the semester began to engage with students as soon as they hit campus. The draw was big. Students who came to our events were attracted by the group dynamic, and they went away wanting to attend more events and to invite their friends the next time.

We didn't host fun events just for the sake of having fun. Our church was mission-oriented, and we purposefully designed our fellowship activities around our mission—to reach college students with the Gospel and to train them in the Word of God to become a Christian generation of change agents who would transform society. We were motivated by the belief that tomorrow's leaders are on the campus today. Each year if we could win students for Christ, grow our influence, and reproduce our efforts at other colleges and universities, we just might be used by God in His grand redemptive work to set all things right. Our staff strategically developed relationships with as many students as possible. We then introduced the word of God into those relationships through weekly Bible studies. The fellowship activities were a great way to meet large numbers of students, begin to develop those relationships, and then establish evangelistic and discipleship Bible studies with them. Students who connected with our ministry intuitively sensed our commitment to mission—and were drawn to it.[7]

As Dr. Barna's research shows, people want to be part of something that is bigger than themselves—to "be the change," to "make a difference."[8] And this is particularly true among young people. But we didn't take it for granted that students would catch our vision and embrace our mission. We were intentional to foster that in them.

As soon as students received Christ, we encouraged them to share their brand-new faith with their friends, to join us in other evangelistic Bible studies where they could tell their testimonies and go out with our evangelistic staff to witness to students in impromptu conversations on campus. They often saw others receive Christ through these efforts and the flame of mission would be kindled within them. We encouraged students who had trusted Christ to begin praying for their friends, classmates, and the people living in their dorms and to look for opportunities to invite them to a Bible study or to church. We held Saturday night prayer meetings where hundreds of students, staff, and lay church members would spend time worshiping God and then would pray for the salvation of those being reached through our evangelistic efforts. Each week there were testimonies of God working in these students' lives, adding to the fervency of our prayers for those who still needed a breakthrough. On Sunday mornings, we would go to the dorms and give requested wake-up calls to students who said they wanted to attend church. Scores of students could be seen walking in groups from the dorms to attend church on campus. To see hundreds of college students worshiping God with hands lifted to heaven was captivating. The sense that God's Kingdom was advancing on our campus was palpable and contagious.

For spring break, our staff organized and led evangelistic outreaches to other universities with a different week off. We loaded into several rented 15-passenger vans and spent hours driving to San Diego State University, or University of Southern California, or University of Nevada Las Vegas, or some other school. The travel time was fun, as we deepened our relationships and anticipated how God would use us to see lives changed during the week. We ate our meals together, went out in pairs on the campus to share the Gospel, performed evangelistic skits in the middle of campus, and preached open-air throughout the week. Each night we gathered and heard testimonies of those who had received Christ that day. By the end of the week, we had collected hundreds of names of students who had expressed an interest in a Bible study or attending church and shared those with our host church for follow-up. Many times, students who had sacrificed their spring break to tell others about Jesus heard a call from God to go into full-time ministry. We always ended the week on a celebratory note, going to the beach or to a fun place like Universal Studios.

Beyond the sense of mission and purpose, the experience fostered an authenticity of relationship and community. It's hard not to be authentic when you spend a week with 30 to 50 people, sharing every meal, sharing sleeping and bathroom space, and serving one another. You see it all—the good, the bad, and the ugly. And you work out your issues with humility, grace, and repentance. But you know you're in it together, that you're part of a team that has your back, and that God is in your midst, working through you for His purposes.

My wife and I also wanted to demonstrate authenticity in more ordinary and routine ways by including students in our everyday lives. We regularly hosted students for dinner or invited them to spend time in our homes where they could see our marriage and kids up close. We avoided appearing as the perfect family with no problems. We knew that being real reached students with teachable moments for discipleship and gave them a vision for their futures. We look back on our time in student ministry with fondness. Just writing down these memories has rekindled my passion for seeing a generation won for Christ and discipled to be His ambassadors to a world that is desperately hurting for answers.

Even though I'm no longer in campus ministry, God still has me on the university campus, and I continue to see the importance of authentic community and purpose among Millennials. I began teaching in 2013 in the Department of Biblical and Theological Studies at Arizona Christian University. This was just a few years after Len Munsil had become president. He led the effort to transform a small Bible college (then Southwestern College) into a liberal arts university with a strong mission to provide "a biblically-integrated, liberal arts education equipping graduates to serve the Lord Jesus Christ in all aspects of life, as leaders of influence and excellence."[9] The University has an equally strong vision "to educate and equip followers of Christ to transform culture with truth." Students who come to ACU are encouraged to embrace this mission and vision as their own. In fact, this begins in the very first class freshmen take.

I've taught this introductory freshman course—LIA 101: C3: Community, Covenant, Commitments—on multiple occasions, and it is part of ACU's CORE curriculum. The course introduces students to what ACU is all about—its history, mission, vision, community covenant, Core Commitments, the philosophy behind our liberal arts education, and the strategy of our academic programs. Students read and engage with President Munsil's book, *Transforming Culture with Truth*, where they learn that our degree programs are designed to launch graduates into what some have referred to as the seven spheres (or mountains) of cultural influence—religion, education, business, government, media, arts and entertainment, and family.[10] This concept provides a strategic framework for realizing ACU's vision to transform culture with truth as graduates move into their careers as leaders of influence and excellence in these various areas.

Other course assignments help instill a sense of mission and purpose. Students read *StrengthsFinder 2.0* by Tom Rath[11] and identify their top five strengths. With these in mind, they are assigned a "purpose paper" as they begin to identify what their God-given purpose for life might be. This foundational course sets students on a path of discovery that will lead them through the rest of their years at ACU. It begins to create in them a sense that God has called them to be part of His bigger plan for the world—and that they play a unique role in that plan.

Another aspect of ACU's curriculum is designed to give students a sense of purpose and a captivating understanding of God's metanarrative for redemption that is cosmically bigger than the over-individualized and myopic version of the Gospel message typically presented in the Western church. Certainly, the church should preach personal salvation. This is an essential aspect of first importance in the gospel proclamation. But I believe God wants the church to proclaim His even bigger plan and purpose for *all* of creation. As I work with Millennials, they seem largely unmoved by a message of individual salvation in the "sweet by and by." But they will be attracted to this bigger purpose and metanarrative: God's plan seeks human flourishing and reclamation of society and the world— beginning with the here and now, and continuing in the age to come.

To accomplish this, the ACU Academic division began revamping our 18-credit Bible minor in 2018 to better connect with students. We discovered our Bible minor was based on an academic model that was at least 150 years old. It assumed a fairly high level of biblical literacy on the part of incoming students.[12] For several years, our Bible faculty recognized we could no longer assume students came to us with that same foundation of biblical knowledge.[13]

Then-Academic Dean Dr. Edward Clavell led a team of faculty to address the task of how to teach the Bible in a way that connects with students who may have little or no prior biblical knowledge, but that doesn't sacrifice academic rigor. We knew we wanted a curriculum that brought the biblical metanarrative of Creation, Fall, Redemption, and New Creation to life for our students. Through a collaborative process, we created four courses to help students see God's metanarrative unfold from Genesis to Revelation. We were careful to incorporate two pedagogical approaches, the biblical theology model and systematic theology. And we settled on four main themes—the divine covenants, the image of God, the temple and tabernacle, and the kingdom of God. To complete the 18-hour Bible requirement, these four core courses would be bookended with a course introducing the Bible and an upper-division Bible elective.

The collaborative fun, excitement, anticipation, and academic exhilaration we all felt in the creative process was magnified once we began offering the courses. The positive impact was immediate. As I taught my course on the covenants for the first time, I was thrilled to see "lightbulbs going off" in my students. The feedback from students? The Bible made sense to them in a way it never had before. Even students who had a relatively strong Bible background said for the first time, they saw how the Old Testament fits with the New Testament. They were seeing how the various parts of the Bible fit together in a way that testifies to its supernatural origin as a divinely inspired work. But perhaps most satisfying, students were seeing how Scripture connects practically with their own lives and how they personally fit within God's plans for creation and redemption.

I am more encouraged than ever that the church and Christian educators have the answers to the challenges that Millennials face. Dr. Barna's research provides us with invaluable insights into these challenges. On first reading, the picture looks bleak. But I believe the Holy Spirit can guide God's people to meet the challenge. My prayer is that the ideas in this book will provide insights and suggestions to that end, and I hope my contribution adds to the effort—to engage Millennials with authentic community that inspires purpose.

We all have a part to play. Pastors, preachers, youth ministers, and Bible study leaders are my heroes. You should never stop proclaiming the need for repentance and belief in the Gospel of Jesus Christ for personal deliverance from sin and eternal life. But let's also wrap into our proclamation a more fully orbed presentation of God's plan of reclamation for all creation—including how He is at work transforming every area of society and culture. Let's embrace strategic missions and visions, bathed in prayer, which can be translated into concrete action plans for the people in our churches to get engaged. Let's be intentional about every church function and event we sponsor, considering how it helps advance each church's God-given mission.

Pastors and elders, let's be intentional and active in helping our people discover their gifts and talents, and creatively provide opportunities for them to use those gifts to further God's kingdom. Then let's release them and help them move into their unique ministries.

Youth pastors and young adult leaders, let's try to avoid planning events that simply entertain and provide social engagement for those already in the church. Instead, let's be strategic and turn these events into evangelistic outreaches that challenge and inspire our people. To be a place where the lost can find authentic community and be inspired to contemplate their purpose in God's big picture.[14] Let's move beyond just engaging with people on Sundays. Instead, let's all (vocational ministers and lay leaders) bring young adult singles and couples into our homes and into our lives—so that they can see authentic relationships, marriages, and families, and offer a vision for their futures. Despite the temptation to settle for the comfort of what God has already done—we may miss the new thing He is doing today that might challenge and stretch us.

Christian educators, I praise God for you. Never lose your passion for seeing the lights go on in your students. Perhaps you resonate with ACU's faculty, concerned about the decreasing biblical literacy within the next generation. Let's be innovative in our approach to biblical education and work to present the timeless message of Scripture in fresh and captivating ways. Let's communicate with one another and cross-pollinate ideas. We'd love to hear ways that you have addressed the challenges of educating Millennials—and now Gen Zers—who are in our institutions.[15]

Above all, let us never grow weary in well-doing. We serve a God who makes all things possible.

Notes

1. George Barna, *Millennials in America* (Part 1 of this text), 61-62.

2. Barna, *Millennials in America*, 29.

3. R. York Moore, "Search: Reaching Millennials with the Gospel 2017," https://www.youtube.com/watch?v=JOoVdiC0V3c&t=1334s.

4. See for example, N.T. Wright, *Justification* (Downers Grove, IL: IVP Academic, 2009), 164.

5. JoAnna Dias, "Millennials in Relational and Mental Health Crisis," Millennial Panel 2, Voice of Reason, Foundations of Freedom, Jan.10, 2022. Accessed at: https://www.arizonachristian.edu/culturalresearchcenter/resources/ Dr. Dias' expanded remarks are included her contribution to this text, "A Christian Formational Approach to Supporting Millennials," 109-126.

6. Barna, *Millennials in America*, 20.

7. This accords well with John Stonestreet's comments in the first Millennial Panel discussion. He said that "Worldview is far more often *caught* than *taught*." See: "Creating Strategies to Reach a Generation in Crisis," Millennial Panel 1, *Voice of Reason*, Foundations of Freedom, November 17, 2021. Accessed at: https://www.arizonachristian.edu/culturalresearchcenter/resources/.

8. Barna, *Millennials in America*, 30.

9. More information about Arizona Christian University's conservative Christian mission and vision can be found on its website: https://www.arizonachristian.edu/.

10. Len Munsil, *Transforming Culture with Truth*, Second Edition (Glendale, AZ: Arizona Christian University Press, 2020), 154. The concept of the seven mountains or spheres of cultural or societal influence was developed by Bill Bright, founder of Campus Crusade for Christ, and Loren Cunningham, founder of Youth with a Mission. See: "Influencing Culture: The Seven Mountains of Culture," Pinnacle Forum website, available at: https://pinnacleforum.com/about/.

11. Tom Rath, *StrengthFinder 2.0* (New York: Gallup Press, 2007).

12. At the time, ACU's required Bible minor consisted of 18 credits, including six courses: an introduction to the Bible course, a course in biblical interpretation, a semester each of Old Testament survey and New Testament survey, a systematic theology course, and an upper-division elective. The current Bible minor still requires all students to complete 18 hours of Bible credit.

13. I believe this phenomenon comports with and possibly explains many aspects of Dr. Barna's findings in *Millennials in America*. For example, low knowledge of Scripture helps explain why Gen Xers and Millennials can embrace

a belief in God that is more in line with Moralistic Therapeutic Deism than biblical Christianity. See Barna, *Millennials*, 67.

14. An excellent resource with suggestions for how to do this can be found in Sean McDowell and J. Warner Wallace, *So the Next Generation Will Know: Preparing Young Christians for a Challenging World* (Colorado Springs, CO: David C. Cook, 2019).

15. I can be reached at: jeff.phillips@arizonachristian.edu.

Appendix

Helping Millennials Thrive:
Practical Wisdom for a Generation in Crisis

———

About the Research

Millennials in America: New Insights
into the Generation of Growing Influence

Research by George Barna

Millennials In America: New Insights into the Generation of Growing Influence – A Research Report by George Barna, Cultural Research Center at Arizona Christian University was originally published by Arizona Christian University Press (2021). It is reprinted in its entirety as Part I of this book.

It is a project of Foundations of Freedom, a peer-to-peer platform where believers in traditional American Values unite, maximizing our collective influence and impact on society. The research was commissioned by Foundations of Freedom to understand our youngest generation at a deeper level.

It is a joint project with the Cultural Research Center at Arizona Christian University, which exists to advance the Kingdom of God by conducting culture and worldview studies that provide research and resources to inform and mobilize strategic engagement in cultural transformation. We thank Foundations of Freedom for their generous support of this research.

Research Methodology

The survey was developed and implemented during August 2021 for Foundations of Freedom. The research objective was to obtain insights into the Millennial generation, defined as all adults born from 1984 through 2002. The survey question modules were developed to explore aspects of lifestyle, politics, faith, relationships, and emotional conditions. The information was garnered to be shared with the public in the hope of educating people about Millennials; motivating them to be supportive of the generation; and activating those people in practical and tangible ways.

Toward that end, a survey questionnaire was developed, tested, and deployed with a nationwide sample of the general public, aged 18 and over. Individuals who fit within the Millennial age bracket (18 to 37 years of age at the time of the survey) were qualified to complete the survey. The sampling and data collection procedures were designed to provide a base of respondents whose basic profile reflected that of the Millennial population in relation to factors such as geographic dispersion, race, and gender.

The data were collected using online capabilities. The survey questionnaire contained 71 questions. The median length of a completed survey was 17 minutes. The 600 survey respondents were promised anonymity and that their answers would remain confidential.

The research was developed, managed, and analyzed by the Cultural Research Center at Arizona Christian University, a non-profit research institute associated with the university. The research was led by Dr. George Barna, a professor at the university and Director of Research for the Center. The Cultural Research Center, which specializes in research related to worldview and to cultural transformation, is located on the university's campus in Glendale, Arizona, which is in the Phoenix metropolitan area. For more information about the Center, or to access reports based on its research, visit the Center's website at www.culturalresearchcenter.com.

Some of the questions and data appearing in this study have been drawn from the *American Worldview Inventory*, an annual nationwide assessment of worldview conducted by the Cultural Research Center; that information was used with the permission of the Center.

About the Researcher

George Barna is a professor at Arizona Christian University (ACU) and co-founded the Cultural Research Center, based at the University. His focus at ACU is worldview assessment and development, and cultural transformation. He was the founder and leader of The Barna Group (which he sold in 2009) and the American Culture and Faith Institute (2011-2018). He has been the President of Metaformation, a research and communications company, since 2009. Barna serves as the Senior Research Fellow for the Center for Biblical Worldview at the Family Research Council. He is also a Fellow at the Townsend Institute, associated with Concordia University.

Barna has conducted groundbreaking research on worldview, cultural transformation, ministry applications, spiritual development, and election strategy. He has provided research strategy to several hundred parachurch ministries, thousands of Christian churches, the U.S. military, and numerous non-profit and for-profit organizations, and has provided polling and strategy input for four presidential candidates.

Barna has written or co-authored more than 50 books, mostly addressing cultural and religious trends, leadership, spiritual development, church dynamics, and cultural transformation. They include *New York Times* bestsellers and several award-winning books. His books have been translated into more than a dozen languages. He lists his most influential books as *The Frog in the Kettle, Transforming Children into Spiritual Champions, Revolution, Think Like Jesus, Pagan Christianity*, and *Maximum Faith*. His most recent books are part of the *American Worldview Inventory* series.

Before his current role at Arizona Christian University, he taught at several universities (Pepperdine University, Azusa Pacific University, Biola University, and Dallas Baptist University) and seminaries (including Reformed Theological Seminary, Talbot, and others). He has been the teaching pastor of a large, multi-ethnic church, pastor of a house church, and an elder at three churches. An in-demand public speaker, Barna has spoken at hundreds of public events during his career. He is also a frequent guest on media programs, discussing his research findings and their implications.

After graduating summa cum laude from Boston College with a degree in Sociology, Barna earned two master's degrees from Rutgers University and received a doctorate from Dallas Baptist University. Born in New York City, he married his wife, Nancy, in 1978. They have three daughters and three grandchildren. They live on the central California coast and in the Phoenix area.

About the Cultural Research Center at Arizona Christian University

The Cultural Research Center (CRC) at Arizona Christian University was launched in March 2020 to conduct cutting-edge cultural and biblical worldview studies to provide credible research and resources to inform and mobilize strategic engagement in cultural transformation. The starting point of transforming culture is to get a clear picture of the worldviews that animate its landscape.

The Cultural Research Center at Arizona Christian University is located on the school's campus in Glendale, Arizona, in the Phoenix metropolitan area. In addition to conducting the annual *American Worldview Inventory*, CRC also introduced the *ACU Student Worldview Inventory (SWVI)* in 2020. That survey is administered to every ACU student at the start of each academic year, and a final administration among students just prior to their graduation.

The *ACU SWVI* enables the University to track the worldview development of its student body and to make changes to the educational process as suggested through the research. The Cultural Research Center also conducts nationwide research studies to understand the intersection of faith and culture and shares that information with organizations dedicated to transforming American culture with biblical truth.

CRC is guided by George Barna, Director of Research, and Tracy Munsil, Executive Director. Like ACU, CRC embraces biblical Christianity. The Center serves alongside a variety of theologically conservative Christian ministries and remains politically non-partisan. Access to the results from past surveys conducted by CRC, as well as additional information about the Cultural Research Center, are available at www.culturalresearchcenter.com.

The goal of the Cultural Research Center is to become the nation's primary biblical worldview hub. Arizona Christian University will continue to provide worldview education to college students, but that activity is just one of the many that relate to the core mission of ACU—expanding the biblical worldview in America—both in the Church and in American culture.

As the biblical worldview research and resource arm of Arizona Christian University, the Cultural Research Center provides research and resources to individuals, families, churches, schools and universities, and organizations that seek to strategically increase the level of biblical worldview among people of faith and within American culture.

The Cultural Research Center also collaborates with other leading national organizations, with the goal of providing reliable research and effective resources for biblical worldview understanding within all areas of American culture.

The Cultural Research Center serves Arizona Christian University's worldview development efforts by measuring student worldview development using the *ACU Student Worldview Inventory* (administered throughout each student's academic career). ACU is committed to biblical worldview development and assessment in all facets of the student experience.

The Cultural Research Center team includes:

George Barna, CRC Director of Research. Barna is the nation's leading researcher in the area of faith and culture. He co-founded the CRC as its Director of Research and is a professor at Arizona Christian University. He also founded the Barna Group (which he sold in 2009), a research company that has set the standard for understanding trends in American culture. Barna has written more than 50 books, including numerous award winners and *New York Times* bestsellers. His full bio is available on p. 224.

Tracy F. Munsil, Ph.D., CRC Executive Director. Dr. Munsil is an Associate Professor of Political Science at Arizona Christian University. She created the University's political science program and chaired the ACU Department of Government, History and Philosophy for eight years prior to becoming CRC Executive Director. Dr. Munsil also chaired the collaborative process to develop the ACU CORE, which integrates biblical worldview into the University's distinctive liberal arts curriculum. She developed a passion for biblical worldview while home-educating her eight children for 14 years. Her Doctorate in political science in 2011 was her third degree from Arizona State University, after earning both a political science master's and a bachelor's degree in journalism. In addition to her work as CRC's Executive Director, Dr. Munsil also serves as Editor of Arizona Christian University Press. She was appointed by Arizona Governor Doug Ducey and confirmed by the Arizona Senate for two terms on the Arizona Commission on Appellate Court Appointments.

CRC interns Abigayle Fesmire and Macy Spengler assisted on this project. Arizona Christian University Press intern Savannah Smith assisted with the proofreading of the final text.

About Arizona Christian University

Arizona Christian University (ACU) is an accredited, private, non-profit, Christian university in the Phoenix metropolitan area. ACU is an award-winning, culturally and theologically conservative university where students and their professors are serious about deepening their Christian faith and where relationships and community deeply matter. It offers a wide variety of degrees preparing students for successful careers, while remaining committed to its vision of transforming culture with biblical truth. Students actively engage in biblically-integrated academics and gain a liberal arts foundation with critical thinking skills that last a lifetime. Spiritual development is integrated within the University experience, where all four-year campus students receive a minor in Biblical Studies, attend chapel twice a week, and complete spiritual formation and service hours each semester.

Led by President Len Munsil, Arizona Christian University is one of the fastest-growing Christian universities in America and ranked by *U.S. News & World Report* as the No. 1 Undergraduate Teaching Institution in the West. Arizona Christian University provides a biblically integrated, liberal arts education equipping graduates to serve the Lord Jesus Christ in all aspects of life as leaders of influence and excellence. Arizona Christian University exists to educate and equip followers of Christ to transform culture with the truth.

Further information about Arizona Christian University is available at www. arizonachristian.edu.

Resources

Research

Millennials In America: New Insights into the Generation of Growing Influence – A Research Report by George Barna, Cultural Research Center at Arizona Christian University, was published by Arizona Christian University Press, 2021.

It is reprinted in full as Part I of this book (pp. 1-77) and also available as a digital resource at the website of the Cultural Research Center at Arizona Christian University (www.CulturalResearchCenter.com) and at Foundations of Freedom (www.FoundationsofFreedom.com).

Millennial Panels based on Millennials in America research:

Four Millennial Panels provided the impetus this resource, *Helping Millennials Thrive: Practical Wisdom for a Generation in Crisis* (Arizona Christian University Press, 2023). The panels featured national experts and ministry leaders discussing the findings of the Millennials in America research. They were hosted by Foundations of Freedom and the Cultural Research Center at Arizona Christian University, and featured presentations from CRC Director of Research George Barna and were hosted by Len Munsil, President of Arizona Christian University.

Millennials in Spiritual Crisis and Loss of Biblical Worldview (01-31-2022)
Featuring: Che Ahn, Dr. Jeff Myers, Isaac Crocker, Samuel Rodriguez, and Dr. Jeff Phillips

Millennials Seeking Meaning and Purpose (01-17-2022)
Featuring: John Stonestreet, Dr. Jeff Myers, Dr. Tim Clinton, Lucas Miles, and Dr. Raleigh Washington

Millennials in Relational and Mental Health Crisis (01-10-2022)
Featuring: Dr. Ken Sande, Dr. John Townsend, Garry Ingraham, and Dr. JoAnna Dias

Creating Strategies to Reach a Generation in Crisis (11-17-2021)
Featuring: John Stonestreet, Dr. John Jackson, Ché Ahn, Dr. Raleigh Washington, Samuel Rodriguez, and Garry Ingraham

They are available on the Resources page of the Cultural Research Center website (https://www.arizonachristian.edu/culturalresearchcenter/resources/)

Books

Anderson, Kristen Soltis. *The Selfie Vote: Where Millennials Are Leading America*. Northampton, MA: Broadside Books, 2015.

Barna, George. *American Worldview Inventory 2020-2021*. Glendale, AZ: Arizona Christian University Press, 2021.

Boucher, Debbie. *Millennial Fears*. Portland, OR: Outskirts Press, 2011.

Burstein, David. *Fast Future: How the Millennial Generation Is Shaping Our World*. New York, NY: Beacon Press, 2014.

Cairns, John. *The Myth of the Age of Entitlement: Millennials, Austerity, and Hope*. Toronto, ON: University of Toronto Press, 2017.

Filipovic, Jill. *Ok Boomer, Let's Talk: A Millennial Defense of Our Generation*. NY: Atria/One Signal Publishers, 2020.

Fletcher, Michael. *The Millennial Manifesto*. Self-published: Toronto: ON, 2019.

Freedlander, David. *The AOC Generation: How Millennials Are Seizing Power and Rewriting the Rules of American Politics*. New York, NY: Beacon Press, 2021.

Howe, Neil and William Strauss. *Millennials Rising: The Next Great Generation*. New York, NY: Vintage Books, 2000.

McFarland, Alex and Jason Jimenez. *Abandoned Faith: Why Millennials Are Walking Away and How You Can Lead Them Home*. Colorado Springs, CO: Focus on the Family, 2017.

Petersen, Anne Helen. *Can't Even: How Millennials Became the Burnout Generation*. New York, NY; Mariner Books, 2020.

Scott, Shaun. *Millennials and the Moments That Made Us: A Cultural History of the U.S. from 1982-Present*. Portland, OR: Zero Books, 2018.

Seel, David John. *The New Copernicans: Millennials and the Survival of the Church*. Nashville, TN: Thomas Nelsons, 2018.

Skeldon, Grant. *The Passion Generation: The Seemingly Reckless, Definitely Disruptive, But Far From Hopeless Millennials*. Grand Rapids, MI: Zondervan Books, 2018.

Smith, Christian and Melinda Todd Denton. *Soul Searching: The Religious and Spiritual Lives of American Teenagers*. New York, NY: Oxford University Press, 2005.

Strauss, William and Neil Howe. *Millennials and the Pop Culture: Strategies for a New Generation of Consumers in Music, Movies, Television, the Internet, and Video Games*. Dallas, TX: Course Associates, 2006.

Websites

https://www.CulturalResearchCenter.com

https://www.FoundationsofFreedom.com

Reports and Studies

Making Space for Millennials. Barna Group: Ventura, CA; 2014. Available at: https://www.barna.com.

William Frey. "The Millennial Generation: A Demographic Bridge to America's Diverse Future." Brookings Institute: Washington, D.C. 2018. Available at: https://www.brookings.edu/research/millennials/.

"The Millennial Study." Accel + Qualtrics. 2016. Available at: https://www.qualtrics.com/millennials/.

"Millennials." Pew Research Center. Available at: https://www.pewresearch.org/topic/generations-age/generations/millennials/.

"Millennials." Gallup. Available at: https://news.gallup.com/topic/millennials.aspx.

CPSIA information can be obtained
at www.ICGtesting.com
Printed in the USA
JSHW042319030423
39857JS00006B/115